• HALSGROVE DISCOVER SERIES ➤

NORFOLK

EXPLORING THE LAND OF WIDE SKIES

Daniel Tink & Stephen Browning

HALSGROVE

First published in Great Britain in 2011

British Library Cataloguing-in-Publication Data
A CIP record for this title is available from the British Library

ISBN 978 0 85704 081 7

HALSGROVE
Halsgrove House,
Ryelands Business Park,
Bagley Road, Wellington, Somerset TA21 9PZ
Tel: 01823 653777   Fax: 01823 216796
email: sales@halsgrove.com

Part of the Halsgrove group of companies
Information on all Halsgrove titles is available at: www.halsgrove.com

Printed in China by Everbest Printing Co Ltd

*This wreck at Blakeney has become a
well-known landmark in itself.*

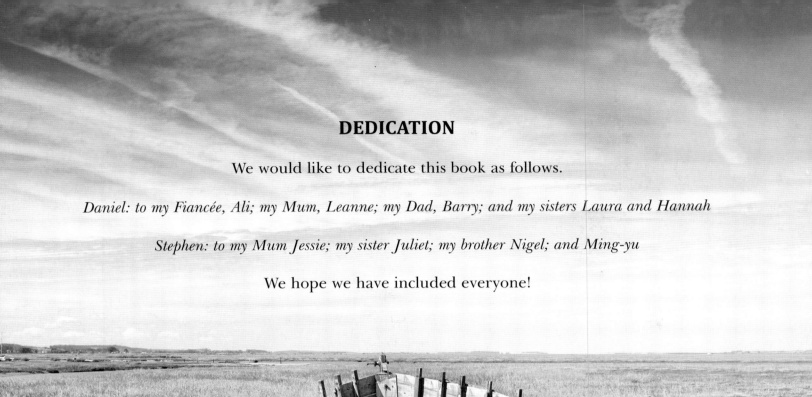

DEDICATION

We would like to dedicate this book as follows.

Daniel: to my Fiancée, Ali; my Mum, Leanne; my Dad, Barry; and my sisters Laura and Hannah

Stephen: to my Mum Jessie; my sister Juliet; my brother Nigel; and Ming-yu

We hope we have included everyone!

CONTENTS

NORFOLK

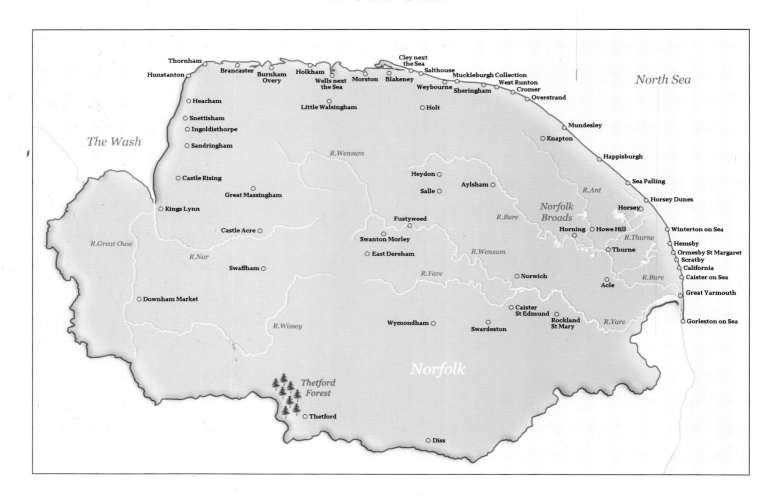

Sunrise at Happisburgh.

ACKNOWLEDGEMENTS
The authors would like to acknowledge the help of
Norfolk historian, David A. Berwick, for his excellent
research into Happisburgh and Mundesley.
David has loved these places all his life.

WHAT MAKES NORFOLK SPECIAL?

*We asked some well-known residents and admirers why they love Norfolk
and this is how they responded.*

Just three reasons why I love Norwich and Norfolk.

1. I can't think of anywhere better to live.

*2. I was brought up in Diss. Left the county in my teens and lived in various parts of the country -
from Dorset to Yorkshire – before returning home. It was the best thing I ever did.*

*3. Yes, the county with its big skies, its Fine City, its market towns and charming villages is special,
but it is the people who are the icing on the Norfolk cake – a rich and tasty collection of folk with a
unique sense of humour.*

Is it the most perfect place on God's earth?

Not far off!

Derek James, Sheriff of Norwich 2010 and Features Editor, *Norwich Evening News*

Norwich
*What a hidden gem is Norwich. It sits in the middle of a piece of land jutting out into the North Sea
with no landfall between it and the North Pole – no wonder the weather is always a favourite topic.
The people have their own character and dialect, different from the rest of Norfolk, sometimes
reflecting our links with those countries across the North Sea with which we traded so long ago.*

*The city itself, once the second most important after London, is full of surprises. Something totally
unexpected may greet you as you wander down any narrow street. Yet it also has a busy and vibrant
centre catering for all manner of tastes. I wonder how many other cities can boast over thirty medieval
churches, two cathedrals, a one-time royal castle, be high on the list of best shopping areas and have
its ancient heart still beating?*

*A sailing boat at Burnham
Overy Staithe awaits the ebb
and flow of the tide.*

Norwich is a lovely place to live and also to visit. So seek us out if you don't know us. I know you will not be disappointed.

Jan King, Blue Badge Guide

As a photographer, although not a Norfolk man, I have viewed the County of Norfolk with the eyes of an outsider. This has given me the opportunity to cover the county with my camera and to find that it is a place of such varied beauty. Norfolk, flat? It is certainly not! At least not completely. Where the terrain is flat the skies take over with stunning cloud formations and wonderful light; where the Broads give a never ending place to enjoy the man-made lakes and natural waterways. Go to coastal areas such as Cromer and Sheringham and the rolling countryside gives one a new perspective and the joy of ever changing views. The sun rises over water at Yarmouth and Gorleston then sets over water at Heacham and Hunstanton, both sunrise and sunset giving the photographer the chance of capturing those softly changing colours at the start and end of each day. With or without a camera, Norfolk is a beautiful county to explore with its wealth of countryside and its fascinating history.

Terry Burchell, Photographer

I love Norfolk because of the beautiful countryside, surrounded by a varied and attractive coastline, the City of Norwich and the lovely unspoilt market towns, the slower pace of life, the people, and the fact that Norfolk is a destination county and not a cut through on the way to anywhere else.

Mike Butler, Jarrold Book Dept, Norwich

One of the joys of Norfolk is that it seems inexhaustible in its interest. Just when you think you have seen all it has to offer you stumble across a new stretch of landscape or a new village or a building or church that you never knew about. That's partly because it is a very large county and contains such a wide variety of terrains, waterways and flora but also because of its history of isolation so there are still remote and untouched areas. It is partly also because of the long tradition of agriculture and land that has been quiet and quietly cultivated for centuries.

I do think you have to bring something to Norfolk in order to appreciate it. It's not a place that throws its charms at you, or that you understand with a quick visit. You have to learn how to look and how to read it and know something about its history. Then you develop an active, and eventually deep, relationship with all the various places that you know, and that makes it personal for every individual and makes you value it far more. I think that's why people stay, and why they come back.

Victoria Manthorpe, Administrator Norwich Society

Norwich is my city of birth and I've come to love its rich historic past, and to delight in the fact that so much of great interest is still available to discover and enthuse over today. The county appeals to me in several ways. The wandering lanes, which often link up with quaint villages, and which nearly always reward the visitor with sight of one of the county's stunningly beautiful medieval village churches, of which Norfolk is blessed with the largest total of any county. There is also something deeply soul-stirring in the county's wide-sky landscapes, whether they are viewed from inland on open heath, or as cliff-top panoramas at any of the many charming coastal resorts. Of course I'm biased, but I feel that Norfolk does 'different' rather well.

David A. Berwick, local historian and writer

Childhood memories of growing up in a county of wide open spaces and big blue skies, under a bright summer sun. The privilege of working at iconic buildings such as Blickling Hall and Norwich Cathedral. Relaxing times listening to the whisper of the reeds whilst watching the sun set by Cley Mill. Walking on a cold winter's day at Blakeney. Norfolk – there is nowhere I would rather be.

Sue Ball, Operations Manager, Norwich Cathedral

Roots and skies – that's why, for me, there's nowhere like Norfolk! I am a product of generations of yeomen and agricultural labourers; and the clear light of those wide, uninterrupted skies reveals the splendour of a goodly heritage.

Revd Jack Burton, Sheriff of Norwich 1988

Dawn: the rising sun casts a pink glow over Morston Harbour.

COMPETITION WINNERS

The authors also held a competition on www.scenicnorfolk.co.uk for the best quotes from Norfolk citizens as to what makes the county so well loved. In the end, we had to award a joint first prize – publication of the quote and a signed copy of 'The Spirit of Norwich' by Daniel Tink – as both of the following were very special. Many congratulations to Sandy Watson and Anna Ovenden!

I love Norfolk for so many reasons. When I first moved here from London I soon became a single parent. Norfolk has given both my son and I so many opportunities that perhaps may not have been provided for in London.

I simply adore the rural villages dotted throughout our North Norfolk Coastline.

I love the expanse, wilderness, big skies, freedom and all the wonderful characters that make Norfolk such a great place to live in.

I love the many redundant churches, old ruins, castles, museums, fishing villages, the slower pace of life, the ability to breathe non-toxic fumes, etc.

Thank you Norfolk for giving me so much.

Sandy Watson, from Thurgarton, Norfolk

Norfolk is a beautiful County offering a lifestyle that most people dream about. The Norfolk Coastline stretches for miles offering sandy beaches and scenic views. You can enjoy the coast and countryside as well as fun and culture in the City of Norwich. Where else would you find paradise? That is why we moved to Norfolk.

Anna Ovenden, from Knapton, Norfolk

INTRODUCTION

'Very Flat, Norfolk'
Noel Coward

OLD CLEVER-CLOGGS, Noel Coward, was not one to let inconvenient facts get in the way of a well-crafted aphorism as his comment on our county demonstrates. It implies that this is really all there is to say about the place. And yet, from a different perspective it is a wise statement because any description of Norfolk has to be limited in scope: the skies are vast; the ocean is immeasurable; the people are hardy; the easterly wind on the North Norfolk Coast can rip through any articles of clothing; and, yes, Noel, the land *is* flat in places. But it is not possible to come up with a valid sentence that summarises the character of whole county.

Easier to say what it is *not*. Not one inch of it is twee or chocolate-boxy. It is not a comfortable, sweet place.

Yes, statements can be made about individual towns, themes and areas. The city of Norwich is the most complete medieval city in the Kingdom. The northern coast is beautiful beyond description with some internationally important bird sanctuaries. The Broads are indeed, to quote Ted Ellis, 'a breathing place for the cure of souls'. Ancient Royalty was very partial to the salted herrings of Great Yarmouth. The greatest ever British Admiral, Lord Nelson, gained a first taste for the sea at Brancaster. Cromer crabs are supreme. The range of beautiful churches, laboured on by families as an act of love for generations, are wondrous and compelling. The county has stimulated an incredible amount of great literature – from *The Hound of the Baskervilles* by Sir Arthur Conan Doyle to *The Shrimp and The Anemone* by LP Hartley. And so on.

Some places are complex and contradictory. Take Hunstanton, for example. To start with, it is pronounced 'Hunstan', or 'Sunny Hunny' by the locals who dwell in a state of perpetual optimism. Looking out to sea, at the never ending 'highway to heaven' in hues of pink, orange, silver, green and blue, as the sun sets on a very long evening, is a never-to-be-forgotten experience of peace and stillness. As is the sighting, on lazy hazy summer days, of magical castles and boats in a mirage on the far horizon. Yet the sea can also blast away a pier, and a storm in the Wash, perhaps of tsunami intensity, is said to have swept King John's crown jewels to the bottom of the ocean. At times like this, nature seems to be saying 'take me as I am: you don't have to like me'.

Us locals would not have it any other way. Being a 'bit out of the way', our county, customs, dialect and way of life have never been simple or easy to understand – no slick advertising agency can brand Norfolk as anything other than 'Norfolk'.

That is why we love it so.

The golden sands of Gorleston beach are a family favourite.

DISCOVERING
THE BEST OF NORFOLK

Acle

All OK here

Acle is reputed to be one of the very few Norfolk villages that suffered no fatalities during the Black Death and, even today, it does have a feeling of good fortune about it. Standing on the River Bure halfway between Norwich and Yarmouth, the name may mean 'in the lea of oaks' – many trees were felled for the Elizabethan navy – or 'a place that overflowed'. Situated on the Wherry Line, it is traditional in character and has won several awards such as 'Village of the Year'.

The pretty Acle Railway Station was built in 1883.

In Roman times it was an important port and until the 1970s a centre for livestock.

To see: The church of St Edmund is unusual in having a round tower, atop of which sits an octagonal stage. The oldest part predates Norwich Anglican Cathedral by about two hundred years.

To do: This is prime walking territory either around the village itself or along the surrounding waterways and fields where you will often see beautiful dragon flies. A local booklet is available in the village with suggested routes.

Aylsham

Aylsham, some ten miles north of Norwich on the River Bure, with a population of about 6000, was founded in about 500AD by Aegel: "Ham' simply means 'settlement', hence 'Aegel's settlement'. It became relatively wealthy in medieval times due to the weaving of linen and canvas, though wool, grain, timber and agriculture later took over as chief

Red Lion Street in the historic market town of Alysham.

The church of St Michael and All Angels, Alysham – exceptionally fine.

trades. Henry VIII granted a market once a week and a fair every year: markets have been important to the town ever since.

During the heyday of coaching, the Black Boys Inn was the principal stop between Norwich and Cromer and, for a time, the town boasted two railway stations, now, sadly, both gone.

Today Aylsham is very proud of its 'green' credentials: it became Norfolk's first plastic-bag-free town a couple of years ago and its Tesco Store, built from wood and recycleable materials mainly, is claimed to be the leading building of its type.

To see: The church of St Michael and All Angels, dating from the 13th century, is a large and beautiful Gothic structure with a 98 ft tower that acts as a landmark for miles around.

Aylsham is an ideal base for exploring the Bure Valley and is also close to the grand estates of Felbrigg and Blickling.

NORFOLK

Blakeney Quay, where you may catch a crab or wait for a seal-spotting trip.

Blakeney

*'The Blakeney people stand on the steeple
And crack hazelnuts with a five-farthing beetle.'*
Ancient rhyme

Boats at Blakeney with the quay in the distance.

Blakeney village goes back to the Domesday Book when it was called Snitterley. By all accounts, it was a pretty lawless place where piracy against passing ships was common. As with many villages along this coast, royalty was not an uncommon sight, drawn particularly by the tasty fresh fish that could be had here.

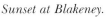

Sunset at Blakeney.

A striking old vessel anchored in the far-reaching marsh at Blakeney.

In 1912, Charles Rothschild bought Blakeney Point and handed it over immediately to the National Trust; thus it became the first nature reserve in Norfolk. It is a three-and-a-half-miles-long sand and shingle spit with incredible wildlife, including both grey and common seals and breeding terns.

To do: There are ferries from Morston Quay which will take you up close to Blakeney Point.

If you like to walk, there is almost no end of choices. Blakeney to Stiffkey – four miles – is popular, or you can plan your own custom-made walk along the North Norfolk Path.

Or try sailing – everything from gentle 'messing about in boats' to serious sea-going challenges are centred at either Blakeney or Morston Quays.

To watch: The man-made vantage point of Mariners Hill is just inland from the harbour.

Brancaster

'I am a Norfolk man and Glory in being so'.
Admiral Lord Nelson, Duke of Bronté

Don't mess with me!
It was here that Nelson as a boy began to mess about in boats before proceeding, later in life, to mess up other people's. His most famous victory, of course, was against the combined French and Spanish fleets at the Battle of Trafalgar in 1805. The county lost its most famous son at the age of 48. Here is an almost contemporary account – it was written in 1822 and comes from *The Norfolk and Norwich Remembrancer and Vade-Mecum*, printed and sold by Matchett & Stevenson, Market Place, Norwich – of how the news reached Norfolk:

'November 7 – Intelligence received of the glorious Victory *obtained over the combined fleets of Spain and France, off Cape Trafalgar, on the 21st of October, though most dearly purchased by the ever-to-be lamented death of Vice Admiral Lord Viscount NELSON, Duke of Bronté, who fell in the arms of victory covered with glory; his memory will be ever dear to the British Navy and the British nation.* The British fleet consisted of 27 sail of the line (three of them 64's), the enemies line of 33 ships (of which 18 were French and 15 Spanish, commanded by Admiral Villeneuve). Nineteen sail of the enemy's fleet struck, and one blew up... Not one of his Majesty's ships were lost... On the receipt of the important news in Norwich, the bells were rung and fired throughout the day; but all the joy that would have arisen from the victory was wholly absorbed in sorrow and regret for the death of the Hero of the Nile and Trafalgar.*

Malthouse Yard Quay provides a base for fishing boats at Brancaster Staithe - try their catch from a fresh fish stall!

*The last order given before the action commenced was by the newly-invented telegraph – "England expects every man to do his duty".

The three villages of Brancaster, Brancaster Staithe and Burnham Deepdale are strung alongside each other on the A149, adjacent to Scolt Head Island Nature Reserve and Brancaster Bay. The settlements are ancient – we know that there was a Roman settlement here, called Branodunum, although to what purpose historians have yet to agree. For many years the villages supported themselves, primarily by fishing and farming, but nowadays many houses are holiday lets.

To see: Just offshore at Brancaster is a petrified forest which can be seen at low tide.

A wreck, once the SS *Vina* and used for target practice by the RAF in 1944, lies visible offshore. Nothing can be done as experts think that the only way to remove it would be by explosives but so much would be required that the operation may well blow up the windows of the houses on the mainland.

Not to see by yourself: The ghost of Nelson's nurse haunts The Ship public house.

To do: You can walk for almost as many miles as you like along the coastal path – it is 47 miles long and heads to Titchwell and Hunstanton in one direction and to Burnham Overy, Holkham and Wells in the other.

The famous Royal West Norfolk golf club was opened in 1892 and is unusual in that it was built on common land and thus the common folk of the area were entitled to use it.

Brancaster Beach - The North Norfolk coast always thrills at sunset.

Sometimes part of it floods, being built on salt marsh, and often it is windy which makes for a challenging game!

Explore the beaches and Scolt Head Island. The island is a bird-watchers' paradise. In 1960, Dr E A Duffey of the Nature Conservancy, East Anglia, wrote that 200 species have been recorded and that the following were regular or irregular breeders:*

Common Tern	Mallard	Blackbird
Sandwich Tern	French Partridge	Song Thrush
Little Tern	Common Partridge	Pied Wagtail
Arctic Tern	Redshank	Yellow Wagtail
Roseate Tern	Lapwing	Swallow
Black-headed Gull	Linnet	Short-eared Owl
Kittiwake	Skylark	Starling
Ringed Plover	Meadow Pipit	Cuckoo
Oystercatcher	Reed Bunting	Stock Dove
Shelduck	Wheatear	

Barrow Common is a popular spot for painters.

To eat: Seafood and, in winter, local Mussels.

Crab and lobster pots sit amongst colourful boats at Brancaster Staithe.

*From *Scolt Head Island*, edited by J A Steers, Professor of Geography in the University of Cambridge; first published 1934, revised edition 1960.

The Broads

'The breathing place for the cure of souls'
Naturalist, Ted Ellis

Boating on the River Bure in the unique wetlands of the Norfolk Broads.

BROADLAND DAYS by Philippa R Miller
Dewdrops, daylight, dawn.
Stillness, sunrise, song.
Chatter, clouds and corn.
Willow, wind and waves.
Racing, ropes and reeds.
Merriment, meanderings.

Sails stowed up at sunset.
Ripples, rest, reflection.
Moonlight, mirages, mist.
Lamplight, lazy laughter.
Silver, silence, stars.
Peace, perfect peace.

Taken from *Norfolk Broads: The Golden Years*
edited by Peter Haining (Halsgrove 2008)

Horsey Windpump is one of many lovely mills to be seen when touring the Broads.

Strange to think that, until the 1960s, The Broads were regarded as natural, not man-made (surely, for one thing, large sections are too straight for the waterways to be have been formed by nature. I used to visit them when I was about nine or ten, before Dr Joyce Lambert had proved that they were dug for the peat, and I always assumed that they were not natural; but then I knew that I was an exceptionally smart boy as my Mummy used to tell me that I was 'too clever by half').

By 'The Broads', or 'Norfolk Broads', people mean the 'Norfolk Broads and the Suffolk Broads'. These comprise about 120 miles of navigable waterways – seven rivers and 63 broads, most of the latter only about around 12 feet deep. They run right into the centre of the county's capital city. Although efforts were made by the merchants of Norwich to use the broads for commercial transport purposes, this was never really successful. They are now used almost exclusively for recreation, the first companies hiring out boats being founded in late Victorian times.

Being the country's largest protected wetland, the birdlife is spectacular – Kestrels, Herons, Geese, Great Crested Grebes, Mallards, Coots, Marsh Harriers, Moorhens and, in winter, Goosanders, all call the area home. Wild plants which, to quote the late Spike Milligan 'intoxicate with their beauty', include Bogbean, Water Mint, Yellow Flag Iris, Marsh Mallow, Marsh Orchid, Reed Mace, Kingcup, Dogrose, Lesser Celandine, Greater Bird's-Foot Trefoil, and Yellow Rattle. This is also one of the very few places where the Fen Orchid can still be found. Folk sometimes remark on the large number of windmills – well, they don't grind anything but are actually wind pumps to help drain the land.

The grass is partly cut and the vegetation kept down by the ultimate 'green' lawn mowers – 24 Konik and Welsh ponies!

To do: Sail! Hire a boat! Three-seater canoes can be hired for around £30 a day from the Broads Authority, as can environmentally friendly electric boats. Walking is difficult in some parts of The Broads, but up to a quarter of a million people 'mess about in boats' every year. It provides a feeling of peace and tranquillity – a sort of 'detachment' from all and sundry on the land – quite unlike anything else.

Go to www.enjoythebroads.com for details of lots of organised events, often free but, if not, inexpensive, such as walks, picnics and bike trails. Some events are very unusual, such as a 'spot a bat and moth' evening.

A sailing yacht and cruiser explore the River Bure in the Norfolk Broads.

Ranworth Broad from the dizzy heights of St Helens Church tower – freely accessible for fantastic views.

Burnham Overy

There are two settlements, Burnham Overy Town – the original (now) small settlement and the larger Burnham Overy Staithe, about a mile away and next to the harbour. To confuse matters, this 'town' is about 1 mile from the larger Burnham Market in one direction and Burnham Thorpe, the birthplace of Norfolk's most celebrated son, Admiral Lord Nelson, Duke of Bronté (the latter title given to him by the King of Italy and not generally alluded to in historical texts), in the other.

Until about five hundred years ago, ships could navigate as far as Burnham Overy Town, but the silting up of the river caused the trade to wither and the coming of the railway to the Burnhams in 1866 killed it altogether.

To do: You can walk about one and a half miles along a footpath from Burnham Overy Staithe to the beach.

Ferries leave from Burnham Overy Staithe to Scolt Head Island Nature Reserve. The harbour is a centre for sailing activities.

A view from the Norfolk Coast Path taking in Burnham Overy Harbour and surrounding Area of Outstanding Natural Beauty.

Wildfowl fly over Burnham Overy Staithe. Winter is a great time of the year to watch vast flocks of birds along the North West Norfolk coast.

NORFOLK

Burham Overy Harbour is scattered with colourful boats - a perfect spot for sailing enthusiasts.

Low tide exposes mud and sands at Burnham Overy Harbour.

Caistor-on-Sea

Three miles from Yarmouth, this attractive seaside resort is reputed to be the most populated village in the UK – approaching 9000 souls. It has sandy beaches and extensive sand dunes.

It also has an amusing claim to fame in that it was the source of some complaints in Victorian times, along with its neighbours, of providing too many Norfolk Dumplings to visitors. Obviously, this saved the landlady spending money on meat, but Norfolk Dumplings are, in fact, a culinary custom in their own right. They are balls of flour and water, thrown into boiling water and cooked for twenty minutes. Fine in stews – as they are never sweet – some households eat them separately with gravy or treacle at the beginning of a meal. It is not considered proper to use a knife and fork, but two forks only, to eat them.

Caistor St Edmund

This village features on Roman maps of the region, which is hardly surprising as it is adjacent to the headquarters of the Iceni tribe, Vente Icenorum. As discussed elsewhere, the Iceni people, and Boudica (it is now considered correct to use this name, although I remember the warrior queen from my schooldays as 'Boadicea') gave the invaders, and locals come to that, much trouble.

Caister St Edmund after snowfall – beautiful at any time of the year.

Fog looms over Caister St Edmund, where the ancient Roman town once existed.

The Bailey Gate is an ancient gateway to the lovely village of Castle Acre.

Wander around the atmospheric remains of Castle Acre.

To see: The lovely church of Caistor St Edmund has witnessed worship for 950 years and is thriving today.

To do: As the photographs show, the scenery around here is beautiful beyond words and perhaps the most worthwhile *'to do'* is ramble. You can organise it yourself or join one of the several rambling trips that take place each year. Details from the Caistor St Edmund website.

Castle Acre

William de Warenne and his wife, Gundreda – daughter of William the Conqueror, no less - were so impressed by the French monastery of Cluny that they brought the Cluniac order to England which resulted in the foundation of Castle Acre Priory in 1090. Along with Castle Acre Castle itself, this now small settlement was once very important and royalty would often be seen here. The monks claimed to have a priceless relic – the arm of St Philip in the reliquary. The present-day ruins are spectacular, and are looked after by English Heritage who have recreated a herb garden as it would have been in medieval times.

Castle Rising

'Rising was a sea-port when Lynn was but a marsh,
Now Lynn is a seaport town,
And Rising fares the worse'

Old Norfolk verse

When I was six and seven, our school bus used to go through Castle Rising. One day, one of the older boys, all a-snigger and a-smutter, told me that Edward II was gay and was put to death in the castle in an unmentionable way with a red hot poker. I could not understand why being happy should cause such trouble.

It is probably bunkum anyway, as he was likely smothered, and the deed was done in Berkeley Castle, not here. However, this was where the new King Edward imprisoned his mother, Isabella, for 28 years having executed her lover, Mortimer, as it was believed that they had instigated his father's murder. She was known as the 'She-Wolf of France' and she is still here, say many. Every full moon a wolf with snow-white fur can be seen prowling the battlements, baying at the moon – this reflects her behaviour in the years

Photograph taken at Castle Rising, with kind permission from the Castle Rising Estate Office, www.castlerising.com

Pretty cottages in Castle Rising.

leading up to her death in 1358 when, Lady Macbeth-like, her conscience ate away at her sanity. Yes, well…

The castle itself is very fine – it is probably modelled on Norwich Castle and it, and the ruined church to the north, date from the same period. With walls up to nine feet thick and three storeys high, the castle would have been an impressive sight from the sea. As the verse at the head of this section laments, Lynn overtook Rising in importance in the mid sixteenth century and the Castle was, for a time, left to rot.

Castle Rising was also, until abolished in 1832, one of the most notorious rotten boroughs in England. This meant that under 900 people – and most of them under the sway of a few powerful ones – could return 2 Members of Parliament at each election. The seats were effectively 'sold' – and you just wasted your money if you tried to contest them. Famous MPs included Samuel Pepys and Sir Robert Walpole, Britain's first Prime Minister.

To see: The Castle and church.

To do: Some delightful walks in the area.

Cley Next the Sea

Cley is not 'next the Sea' at all and has not been for several hundred years, but it once was a very important English port, trading with the Low Countries in agricultural products, fish, coal and cloth.

Nowadays, it earns a living from tourism. Apart from the famous windmill and church, it truly deserves the designation 'Area of Outstanding Natural Beauty'.

To watch: Cley next the Sea is a bird watching site of international importance, all the year round. Here you can see Grey Plovers, Black-tailed Godwits, Spoonbills and several types of waders.

To walk: A walkers' paradise, from the unambitious to the most determined, Cley is on the Norfolk Coastal Path which links to the Peddars Way National Trail at Holme Next the Sea (see 'Peddars Way' section).

Cley Next the Sea is a haven for bird watchers. Here, beyond the reeds, can be seen the beautiful Cley Mill and picturesque village cottages.

Cromer

Cromer Crabs, Runton dabs,
Beeston babies, Sheringham ladies,
Weybourne witches, Salthouse ditches.

Ancient Norfolk rhyme

The Hound of the Cromer Hills
Recovering from enteric fever, Arthur Conan Doyle came to Cromer to recuperate and was told of the legend of Black Shuck, a gigantic hound with eyes that glowed like coals and rumoured to be partial to the throats of local folk who ventured outside after dark. Transferring the action to the chilling loneliness of Dartmoor, possibly the greatest of the Sherlock Holmes adventures was born: *The Hound of the Baskervilles* was published to universal acclaim in several instalments between 1901 and 1902.

Cromer Pier at dusk.

An encounter with The Black Shuck
Later in the same century, Christopher Marlowe, a well-known writer on many things East Anglian, decided to take a cycle tour of the region. He published an entertaining book about his adventures in 1927 (*People and Places in Marshland*, Cecil Palmer, London). It contains the following story. He had been in a pub and casting some doubt about the legend of the Black Shuck. The locals were horrified that he appeared to doubt the truth of the story. He prepared himself, therefore, to spend a night out in an area where the ferocious hound was reputed to roam. Surely he could debunk the myth? Let Christopher take up the story in his own words:

'A yellow half moon was creeping up from the east as I reached my destination and settled down in a hollow, not far from the mark of high tide at 'Stewkey.' A narrow lane led from the marsh proper to the high road some eight hundred yards distant and at the top of this lane gleamed the light from a cottage. I had previously arranged with the owner to spend the night there, and without telling him what I was doing, remarked merely that I might arrive late.

To this he was quite agreeable, but begged me not to venture on the marsh after dark. The Shuck Dog confined his operations to the beds of lavender and never attacked wayfarers on the highway. So I had a certain consolation in the fact that a sprint of eight hundred yards or perhaps a little more would bring me to safety...

...After what seemed a long interval, a gentle sighing came from away by the seashore, some two or three miles off, and the moonlight grew steadily brighter. Then, as I watched from the cover of my hollow, I saw an indefinable shadow, far away on the horizon. At the same moment I heard a sound which brought home to me in a flash the peril of my position. The eerie silence was rent by the most

appalling howl to which I have ever listened – it froze the blood in my veins and caused my hair to stand right on end. And the shadow was coming nearer. Believe me or not, as you will, it may have all been imagination or the result of the tales I had previously heard: but I saw that black hound as clearly as I shall ever see anything again. And I realized that to gain the cottage I had to leave my hiding-place and run up that marshy lane in full moonlight.

As I hesitated, the apparition came closer and I saw that its intention was to approach the pool beside which I was crouching. Its muzzle was to the ground and it was apparently hot on the trail of something or somebody – need I say who that was?

With a yell of terror I jumped from the hollow and fled. Not once did I look behind, but I felt that the creature was in pursuit. Never have I run as I ran that night. Stumbling, cursing, breathing heavily, I tore up the lane and at last gained the threshold of the cottage. With a profound feeling of thankfulness I knocked upon the door and called to the cottager to open. In a moment a light appeared and footsteps descended and came along the passage. Then I heard a welcome voice – " Do yew not be jiffling, sir, I be a-coming."

And as the bolt was undone and the key turned I glanced around to see a pair of ferocious eyes fixed upon me and to feel on my neck a scorching breath. The hound was actually about to spring as the door opened and I fell fainting into the arms of my host. One look he gave and then shut the door with a bang as a great black body seemed to leap through the air and come thudding on the ground outside.'

Christopher rested the whole of the next day before continuing on his cycle tour.

The elegant Cromer Pier as seen from rock pools on the beach.

Cromer sea front on a glorious summer's day.

Healthy air and servants

Cromer is a pretty town with fine shops, museums and restaurants – ideal for an interesting break. One cannot help but see and feel, though, the almost seismic shift that took place in this hitherto gentle settlement of fishermen (called Shipden, the original village now under the sea some small way beyond the pier) in the 19th century. Indeed, some guides actually date its beginnings from this time. It suddenly got 'discovered': the railways came in 1877, as did the future King Edward VII, and writers such as Elizabeth Gaskell wrote about the healthy air. 'Healthy air' to the Brits at this time meant cold, salty and astringent – bracing enough at least to go home and feel good about having a sumptuous meal in the warm. One of the places you could have this was in the Hotel de Paris, originally built as the holiday home of Lord Suffield and converted into a hotel in 1830. For dramatic impact, standing as it does on the top of the cliffs overlooking the wildest sea in the world with the biggest sunsets, it knocked spots off Edward Boardman's Royal Hotel in the county town of Norwich, a rival for well-heeled gentry. Some of the other houses along this coast are almost as grand. They would all have had acres of servants. You cannot help wondering: where did they all come from? (The Midlands, probably). What did they all do in the 'off' season? How did these incomers mix with the pretty penurious locals? Alas, we don't know, but we can wonder and wander.

Reflections of Cromer sea front.

Saving lives at sea

One of the town's most illustrious sons is Coxswain Henry George Blogg who served on the Cromer lifeboat for 53 years. During this time, the lifeboat saved 873 people and Henry Blogg was awarded an incredible 3 Gold and four Silver Medals, as well as the George Cross and the British Empire Medal. He died in 1954. He is, naturally, omnipresent in the town.

To eat:

No doubt, when he was here, Sir Arthur relished the food for which Cromer is now famous – the Cromer Crab, indistinguishable to this impartial observer from the Sheringham Crab, although locals would not thank you for saying so, such is the rivalry between the two towns.

Apple and Crab Coleslaw with fine fresh bread and salad

Combine the following: about half a pound of cooked crab meat; a sweet English apple; a little sugar and vinegar; juice of a lemon; a fair bit of Norfolk cabbage; a few carrots; Norfolk watercress to taste; several tablespoons of French mayonnaise. Mix up.

Serve with a simple salad and fresh bread. A crisp white wine, only slightly chilled, or lemon squash for the kids, complements this light meal perfectly.

Serve ideally on a warm day on your favourite spot overlooking the sea – there are thousands around here. Don't think of the Black Shuck.

To do:

If you like to walk, there are no-end of choices. Taking a walk on the Pier is possibly the gentlest option. There has been a pier or jetty here since the end of the 14th century. Also easy is a walk along the prom and back. For a slightly more energetic walk, it is lovely to walk the couple of miles to Overstrand along the beach, admiring the cliffs and checking out the rockpools, but do be careful to check the tide times at the Information Bureau beforehand. This is, of course, the entry point to the famous Poppyland, so many delights await the walker or cyclist a little farther inland.

Don't do: what The Reverend Benjamin J Armstrong did on April 25th 1878 and take your guests out for a sightseeing stroll when the easterly wind is at its height or you will find them 'filled with grievances' (*A Norfolk Diary*, George G. Harrap and Co Ltd, 1849).

Don't say: to a friendly local 'I think Sheringham is prettier'.

Diss

Diss has been an important town for well over a thousand years partly due to its location on the Norfolk/Suffolk border – in fact, for the first part of its life being officially in Suffolk. It has a fascinating history linked to Lord Fitzwalters, Edward Plantagenet, the Duke of York, Richard the Lionheart, the Earl of Rutland and others who coveted the rich grazing lands around here.

There is a famous little local story which illustrates both the supposed lack of knowledge of the Norfolk people as regards the outside world, and their self-deprecating humour. Not so long ago, a lady from Norwich, no longer young, was about to travel to see her long-lost relatives in Australia. She was warned that the journey was long and arduous. 'Don't you be a'mindin' me', she replied, 'I aim to break my journey in Diss'.

Camping – or 'Kamping' – was a form of medieval football played in East Anglia. The games were played with a bladder filled with dried peas. Many of the county's warriors and strong men would travel miles to take part in these events, which were usually held on a Sunday or holiday. Boots would oftentimes be tipped with horn. In the 1700s a famous Camping match was held at Diss between Norfolk and Suffolk. Normally, up to 24 men took part – this time, there were 300 on each side. The 'ball' was thrown into the middle of the 'pitch' and for a few minutes, people chased it. Then, however, it was lost to sight and a bloody punch up ensued for fourteen hours: nine men died.

Diss Mere is a spectacular focal point set in parkland, with fine views of the village.

By a strange co-incidence, Thomas Lord, founder of Lord's Cricket Ground, where you can witness the gentlest and most gentlemanly of English pursuits, was born here.

Downham Market

Downham Market is an ancient market town, famed in medieval times for butter and horses. The name means 'settlement on a hill'. It is connected to King's Lynn and London by the Fen Line.

Famous residents include Sir Roger Pratt (1620-1684), one of three men – the other two being Sir Christopher Wren and Hugh May – appointed to oversee the rebuilding of London after the Great Fire of 1666. Horatio Nelson attended school here until about ten years old. George Manby, who after witnessing a terrible sea-tragedy dedicated much of his life to inventing devices to save lives at sea, his most famous being the life-saving rocket, was a resident. Charles I, disguised as a parson, had a clandestine meeting in the local hostelry, the White Swan, in 1646 to see if the Scots would support him.

To see: There is the medieval Church of St Edmund and a pretty village sign which depicts his crown and arrows along with two horses indicating the importance of horse trading to the area. A clock tower, built in 1878, stands in the centre of town.

East Dereham

'On an evening of July, in the year 18-, at East D-, a beautiful little town in a certain district of East Anglia, I first saw the light.'

George Borrow, *Lavengro*

The Legend of Princess Withburga
In AD 654, Princess Withburga, youngest daughter of King Anna of the East Angles, founded a religious house in Dereham. During the construction of an accompanying church, she found that she had only dried bread to feed the workmen and no money to buy drink for them. She prayed to the Holy Virgin who, in a dream, told her to send her damsels to a specific place nearby and they would find two does that would provide all the milk necessary to complete future meals. Thus it occurred.

When she died and ascended to Heaven, her earthly body was buried locally. Some years later, her tomb was opened and her body was found to be completely without decay. It was as if she had died that very minute. Her body was taken into the church and revered by the people of Dereham, many miracles taking place around it.

The Danes ransacked the area in 870 and the manor was given to the Abbot of Ely. Now, he became avaricious when he saw the amount of money that pilgrims brought to Princess Withburga's shrine and devised a plan to steal her body and take it to Ely. So,

The Victorian black and white clock tower in Downham Market.

following a session of court justice, he provided a great feast for the people of Dereham which involved heavy drinking and, in the middle of the night, as the people slept off their excess, he and his henchmen stole the body of the Princess.

In Ely, she was once more seen to have no sign of decay upon her, one of the monks producing a maidenly blush on her lovely face as he gently touched her skin. She was interred in Ely Cathedral alongside her sisters Ethelreda and Sexburga and niece, Ermenilda.

As time went on, being only the younger sister and thus outranked by Ethelreda, her tomb was neglected. It cracked. As no-one repaired it she reputedly did so herself. Finally, however, her legend waned and it was even forgotten where she lay. Many visitors to this day search for clues in the Cathedral.

However, in her rightful home town of Dereham, a well miraculously arose on the spot of her original burial. This became a place of pilgrimage which continues now, so a degree of divine justice is served.

Literary connections
A famous son is George Borrow, known for *The Bible in Spain, Lavengro,* and much poetry besides. He was a restless but very friendly soul who soon left the village, voyaging to

This delightful cottage in Dereham dates back to 1502 and was Bishop Bonner's home. It is now a local history museum and holds dark secrets.

46

Spain where, to be honest, the bible does not seem to have a starring role despite the title of his book. It is almost mesmeric, though, in the affectionate way he describes 'ordinary' folk in what was then a strange land of almost unimaginable hardship.

Borrow eventually settled down in Norwich where he would walk for hours upon Mousehold Heath. 'There's a wind on the heath, brother; if I could only feel that, I would gladly live forever', he memorably remarked. He is also responsible for the present proud Norwich slogan 'Norwich, a Fine City'. It was suggested that this be replaced by the altogether charmless and rather rude (to other cities) catchphrase 'Norwich: England's Other City' which, mercifully, has been ditched.

Another famous Downham son is 'England's sweetest' poet, William Cowper (1731–1800), whose gentle nature was easily disturbed. He is one of those poets that most folk know without realising it. Witness: "God moves in a mysterious way, His wonders to perform; He plants his footsteps in the sea, And rides upon the storm."

He also said some amazing things. I like this:
"A fool must now and then be right, by chance."

He has a memorial window in the local church where he is to be seen with his beloved pet hares and dog. His mental state was always fragile. When the lady who loved him, Mary Unwin, died, she was secretly taken away and buried at midnight in order not to upset him. When he later died, he, too, was buried at midnight.

Bishop Bonner's burnings
A man who must have a paragraph to himself so not to contaminate the above two literary figures is Bishop Bonner, remembered now by Bishop Bonner's Cottage Museum. He became Bishop of London in 1540 and later shocked even his most hardened contemporaries by persecuting and burning over 100 Protestants. 'Bloody Bonner' spent the last years of his life in prison when Elizabeth ascended the throne, stubborn to the last.

Dereham, the epicentre of Norfolk, has had an eventful history having suffered several fires and so it presents a mostly Georgian appearance. Until recently there was much light industry, including the Metamec clock factory.

To see: The church dates originally back to Princess Withburga in the 7th century but is largely 13th, 14th and 15th century. It is perfect for contemplation and reflection, being extremely peaceful. There are some lovely Georgian houses in the village.

The bell tower of St Nicholas, Dereham.

Fustyweed

Just to the north of East Dereham, not far from Swanton Morley, is the quintessential Norfolk hamlet of Fustyweed. What a wonderful name! Blink and you'll maybe miss it and end up in the nearby hamlet of Primrose Green but you probably won't mind as all the countryside around here is beautiful. It is an ideal spot to stop the car or bike and take some air. A paradise for bird-watchers, you may spot Sparrowhawks, Grey Herons, Kingfishers, Marsh Tits, Sandpipers, and Fieldfares.

The beautiful countryside around Fustyweed.

Gorleston-On-Sea

Gorleston, great one day will be;
Yarmouth, buried in the sea.
                    Traditional rhyme

Fish and fashionable folk

Gorleston-On-Sea is separated from Great Yarmouth by the River Yare, sitting on the south and west sides. It predates Yarmouth, being important a thousand years ago for the production of salt. Later it became the centre of the herring industry, until early Edwardian times boasting the largest shipping fleet in the world. Neatly dovetailing in as the herring industry shrank, tourism rapidly gained a hold, the town becoming a smart summer destination for fashionable Victorians. Wonderful hotels such as the Pier Hotel (1897), the Cliff Hotel (built 1898 but spectacularly destroyed by fire on a winter's day in 1915) and the Gables Hotel vied with anything Cromer or even Norwich could offer. Such was the money to be made by the rush to the sea, that numerous stories are still told in Gorleston pubs and inns of local people letting out every inch of space in their – often modest – homes and finding sleeping quarters for themselves wherever they could, with relatives maybe, or in tents and sheds. There were three railways stations, alas, now all gone.

To see and do: The town retains an Edwardian elegance while the seafront still has the features that made it so popular a century ago – prom, pier, theatre, yacht pond, cliffs, pretty lawns and tennis courts. The chief glory, though is the Blue Flag sandy beach, one of the finest and cleanest in Norfolk.

The Gorleston (Range Rear) Lighthouse was built in 1878.

Gorleston (Range Rear) Lighthouse stands tall at the mouth of the River Yare.

The Grand Pier Hotel in Gorleston is a stone's throw away from the beach.

Take a look, too, at the two lighthouses. The Gorleston South Pier Lighthouse and Coastwatch station was built in 1955 and doesn't look like a lighthouse at all being an octagonal brick building with tubular steel structures on top. It emits a red flash every thirty seconds. As is the case with some other lighthouses on the Norfolk Coast, it is manned, every day of the year by volunteers. The other is the Gorleston (Range Rear) Lighthouse near the mouth of the river. It is a round tower of brick and was built in 1878. It has two lights, a white – for the harbour entrance – and a red light on top.

Great Massingham

Great Massingham is a small village famous for its ponds and ducks. Like many other Norfolk villages, the name probably derives from the first important family to settle here in the 5th century – the Maersings. There is great community spirit locally with a regular newsletter and organised rambles on many weekends along the large number of footpaths that surround the village.

Like much of Norfolk, Great Massingham's relative isolation from the rest of England ended in spectacular style 1939–45. Our county became the front line of battle. RAF Great Massingham played a significant part in the Second World War, flying Blenheims, Mosquitos and Bostons. Casualties were sometimes heart-breakingly heavy but the sacrifices of these brave men and women will never be forgotten in the local area or farther afield. Many men, especially those from the East – Poles and Czechs – married local girls and stayed on.

Daffodils herald the birth of Spring at Great Massingham.

Great Yarmouth

Yarmouth is an antient town, much older than Norwich; and at present, tho' not standing on so much ground, yet better built; much more compleat; for number of inhabitants, not much inferior; and for wealth, trade, and advantage of its situation, infinitely superior to Norwich.

Daniel Defoe, early 18th Century

History and Herrings

Commonly referred to just as 'Yarmouth', this ancient settlement dates back to at least Roman Times. By the time Henry III granted the town a charter in the 13th Century, the place was wealthy and influential. This had primarily to do with herrings which were famous enough to secure royal approval – Yarmouth was required to send each year one hundred pasties, each containing a herring, to the powers-that-be in Norwich who would, in turn, forward them on to the King. Commoners on holiday could once send a box of bloaters – salted smoked herrings – to their nearest and dearest with a 'wish-you-were-here' note, much like today you can send clotted cream from Cornwall, although I should imagine considerably less popular with the postman, and with those whose letters were transported in the same consignment.

Britannia Pier houses plenty of family attractions including a theatre and funfair.

Wellington Pier and horse drawn carriage rides along the parade.

From 1270 Great Yarmouth held a great forty-day Herring Fair, famous throughout the land. As late as 1890 Hewett's Short Blue Fleet comprised 220 smacks and fish carriers. Whitebait was also a great delicacy – there is no such fish, actually, 'whitebait' being the young and tiny sprats and herrings which travel together in great shoals for safety – and London restaurants could not get enough. Each Whit Monday until the turn of the twentieth century 'The Whitebait Feast' was enjoyed all along the Norfolk Coast.

It is possible that the kipper – a split and smoked herring – was invented by accident. A fisherman by the name of John Woodger had a massive catch of herring in Yarmouth in 1850. He sold some but, not knowing what to do with the rest, he hung them in a hut, kept warm by oak chippings and sawdust, for some days. And Lo! When he returned to sort out his catch, he found he had invented something new to eat. The Bloater was subsequently 'invented' – this is much the same but the complete fish is smoked and also for a shorter time.

Local Victorian recipes for preparing Whitebait included pickling, smoking, boiling, frying, fermenting or eating it raw. The fishes – 'two-eyed steaks' – are extremely nutritious.

A North Norfolk idea for cooking herring is to cut off the head, split open, and simmer in water for about seven/eight minutes: add lemon juice and butter (parsley butter is even better). Alternatively, wipe with Goose fat (left over in Victorian homes as a welcome by-product from Christmas) and griddle or hang above your kitchen fire. As a special treat, cover with boiling beer and leave for thirty minutes: serve with egg sauce and bread.

Woe, woe and thrice woe
The town has also had its fair share of woes – in the First World War it was the first to be attacked by Zeppelin bombardment: in the second it was the last drop-off point for any unused Nazi bombs. Recently, there has been much concern about flooding, 2006 having been particularly bad. Surprisingly, much of historical interest remains – most of the medieval walls and towers, the Tollhouse dating from the 13th century, the oldest government building in the land; and some exquisite Georgian houses. Some would cheekily argue that the new shopping centre, Market Gates, is yet another woe although the range of shops is second only to Norwich.

To do: There are two piers – Britannia and Wellington with the usual seaside attractions plus innumerable amusement arcades. For a traditional British seaside holiday, the 'Golden Mile 'has it all', with fish'n chips aplenty.

Two special features
It is worth a separate look at two features, Firstly, the Winter Gardens, next to Wellington Pier, is a cast iron and glass building, reputedly shipped from Torquay in 1903. Secondly, Nelson's Monument, designed by William Wilkins and situated in South Denes, was completed almost 20 years before the famous column in Trafalgar Square. Today, we tend to think of Nelson primarily as the victor of the world-defining battle of Trafalgar in 1805: this monument, originally proposed as a celebration of the earlier Battle of the Nile, justly brings home the fact that Nelson had many more glories to his name than one battle, however great. It consists of a statue of Britannia erected facing inland, not out to sea; this is not a mistake as many think – Britannia is looking towards Nelson's birthplace of Burnham Thorpe.

To walk: The Golden Mile is flat and easy but can get unremittingly hot on a summer's day, so best put on a hat and lots of sun cream.

To watch: Famous for rare and unusual species of birds and insects, the latter blown over

Amusement arcades provide fun and entertainment along the 'Golden Mile' on Great Yarmouth sea front.

from the continent, plus huge roosts of Mediterranean Gulls and waterfowl, it is really worthwhile to buy a specialist wildlife guide book.

To read: Charles Dickens based much of his own best-loved novel, *David Copperfield*, here, culminating in the most terrifying ocean storm in English Literature. The Elizabethan poet, Michael Drayton, praised the 'sumptuous feast of salted herrings' that could be obtained here (he is most famous for his melancholy lines 'Since there's no help, come let us kiss and part').

Don't read: Anthony Trollope without a sense of humour as he could be quite an old sourpuss about the place, especially in *Can You Forgive Her?* (1864). He is rumoured to have planned the book as an 'antidote' to what he saw as Dickens' absurd enthusiasm for the town.

Happisburgh

'The prevailing wind in Norfolk is onshore; this explains why Norfolkmen invariably speak with their mouths closed.'
   Traditional saying

This is a village that in many ways encapsulates life on the magnificent and untamed North Norfolk Coast. It is a place of great beauty, with fine productive land, and has one of the most beautiful churches in Norfolk. Yet it has also known smuggling, shipwreck, and sometimes great grief, all alongside examples of unfathomable human courage and a refusal to give up in the face of natural and man-made reversals of fortune.

A stubborn limpet
This charmingly discrete coastal settlement grips limpet-like to its sea-threatened cliff top perimeter. As far as we know, it always has. The village name is today pronounced *Hais-brah* and derives from the Old English *Heaps-burgh* meaning Heap's Town.

Fine soil, fine crops
Modern Happisburgh has a population of about 1400 people living in 600 households, according to the 2001 census. Some houses date back to the 16th century. The land around the village, of a rich friable loam, is considered to be of a very high farming quality and produces wheat, barley, turnips, swedes and beans. To a declining extent, fishing also produces income and work for local people.

A very interesting village sign
Just below the church you will find a fine and unusual village sign depicting: Edric the Dane – owner of the land before 1066; Maud, daughter of later landowner, Roger Bigod;

the Revd Thomas Lloyd who, in 1793, held a mass baptism of 170 poor folk, saving them the expense of the party expected by the locals, if you were baptized individually, after such an event; a stalk of wheat, representing fruit of the land; and a lifeboat as Happisburgh life has always been dominated by the ocean.

The sea! The sea!

The vast and uncompromising North Sea looms everywhere in the story of present and past Happisburgh. A terrible storm in 1692 caught over two hundred ships sailing between Wells and Winterton. Perhaps 1000 men perished in one night. On 19 December 1770 *HMS Peggy* foundered on the shore in a NNE squall. Many brave villagers brought carts and horses onto the beach at low water the next day and managed to bring 59 men safely ashore. Alas, 36 more are buried in the churchyard.

The largest ship to be lost off the coast hereabouts was *HMS Invincible*, on Monday 16 March 1801. She was laden with stores and six hundred men and on her way to join Admiral Nelson prior to what was to become the Battle of Copenhagen. She ran aground

NORFOLK

Sunrise at Happisburgh.
Sea defences were erected in a
vain attempt to stop
the forever-invading North Sea.
Sadly, many homes from this
lovely village have lost the
battle against erosion.

on a sandbank off Happisburgh and subsequently sank. Heroic efforts in dreadful conditions saved one hundred and ninety men but as many as four hundred were lost, including the Captain, John Rennie, many bodies being washed-up on the coastline in the ensuing days. One hundred and nineteen men were hastily buried in a mass grave, evidence of which was discovered during excavations in 1988. Later that year, they were at long last given a Christian burial, in the presence of a descendent of Captain Rennie and eight serving members of the modern-day aircraft carrier HMS *Invincible*.

Shipwrecks, brandy and oranges

One of the dubious 'benefits' of shipwrecks was 'sea-bounty'. There were lighter occasions when the residents could not believe their luck when casks of alcohol and other desirable things were washed ashore – once when casks of brandy appeared on the beach, a good time being had by all except for one poor soul who drank himself to death. In 1949, when rationing was at its peak, a most welcome cargo of oranges washed ashore.

Murder will find you out

A legendary tale takes us back to around the year 1800. Three Chinese (but some swear Dutch) sailors-cum-smugglers, fell out with each other over the amount of money they were going to share after selling illegal brandy to the locals. Drinking heavily, they fought and one was killed. The body was dropped down a nearby well.

Not long afterwards a Happisburgh man, Sydney Baker, had been having a few beers at the Hill House pub, and was staggering down the slope back to the village. Moving towards him from the direction of the sea appeared to be a man with no legs and his head dangling behind him, carrying a sack. Sydney struggled home but the next night he, and four friends, went to the well at midnight when the same apparition appeared. Next day the well was found to contain a torso and a sack containing a pair of legs and a head.

The site of the now filled-in well can still be visited about three-quarters of a mile along the B1159 coastal road heading out of the village towards Whimpwell Green.

Elementary my dear Watson

We have already seen the part played by Cromer in *The Hound of the Baskervilles*. This area also inspired Sir Arthur Conan Doyle in another of his famous stories. He came here on a motoring holiday in 1900 and lodged by the Hill House in the Green Room of the adjacent hotel. The landlord's son, Gilbert Cubitt, had devised a way of writing his signature using miniature 'pin men' and this so intrigued Conan Doyle that he weaved it into his story 'The Dancing Men', which was set in and around this part of Norfolk. Interested visitors will find a good deal of Conan Doyle memorabilia is to be found at the Hill House pub.

The magnificent red and white striped Happisburgh Lighthouse built in 1790 is still in operation, and is the only independently operated lighthouse in Great Britain.

To see: The lighthouse, with its 85 foot tower and red and white 'hoops', has served since 1790. Once there was a sister tower 20 feet lower but by 1883 coastal erosion hurried on the task of dismantling it before the sea did the job anyhow. The night-time beam identification is three white light flashes, repeated every thirty seconds. Manned entirely by volunteers, the public – subject to a height restriction – can climb the light's 112 steps on about a dozen occasions during the year. Best to check in advance at www.happisburgh.org/lighthouse.

Happisburgh can also boast a volunteer Coast Watch Station, positioned on the cliff top. It is manned every day of the year and has a sweeping view of about ten miles of horizon and sea. It reports to HM Coastguard at Great Yarmouth.

Another dedicated team will be found at the Happisburgh In-Shore Lifeboat Station at Cart Gap, which is run under the auspices of the Royal National Lifeboat Institution. It relocated in 2002 due to a serious cliff-fall and can now be found at Old Cart Gap.

Also to see 2: The splendidly poised and imposing structure of the 110-foot high church tower church draws your eyes to it even when you are still not within a mile of Happisburgh. Catch the tower on a warm sunny day and it seems to have a golden glow. It has stood here since the 15th century. Sir John Betjeman loved what he saw, and couldn't resist remarking, (no doubt in his usual gleeful way) that the tower was slightly out of alignment with the body of the church itself. No matter, as nothing can take away from this place its just claim to being one of the finest in a county of wonderful churches.

The vicar has more than one flock
As you approach the porch you may well hear the distinctive metallic call of Jackdaws,

who oftentimes hover about the tower's parapets. It is not surprising either on summer days to find that visitors are already arriving ahead of you, ducking past your head and disappearing into the porchway. St. Mary's Church each year prepares for, and welcomes, returning families of swallows, all the way from Africa, who nest in the upper rafters of the porch. The Vicar here does not content himself with one flock! Be sure to close the church door behind you, else birds may follow.

A beauteous stillness

On entering this wonderful place you will discover just how grand and spacious the building is. It is also supremely peaceful. I recently attended a session on poetry at Norwich Cathedral and the words of the Archbishop of Canterbury, Dr Rowan Williams, in describing a slightly different place – a monastery, I think – ring true here: it gives the impression of 'great activity elsewhere'.

Sunrise at Happisburgh.

The font is 15th century craftsmanship of stunning beauty. You will be hard-pressed to find its equal anywhere. The beautiful angels clasping their musical instruments are very fine indeed.

The church itself fell into sad disrepair in the 19th century and extensive remodelling took place, including a completely re-timbered roof of red deal. Work has been continual since then. Donations towards the upkeep of this coastal cathedral, via the Restoration Fund gift box, are always most gratefully received.

Vertigo sufferers avoid at all costs – a 'must do' for others

Fit and bold visitors will enjoy the view from the top of the tower, which is open regularly during summer months. There are one hundred and thirty three steps to the top from where, on a decent day, you can see Norwich Cathedral spire, some 18 miles distant.

Exciting finds

In mid 2010, the BBC announced some results from a six-year excavation on Happisburgh beach. Of international significance, it suggests that man occupied these parts much earlier than previously thought – maybe 970,000 years ago. This was a species of man that has since died out – like us but maybe with a flatter face, not much of a chin to speak of and larger teeth. Further revelations will be fascinating.

Don't expect: Happisburgh does not have, or indeed crave for, the trappings of a seaside resort. It invites you to slow down and let its charm overwhelm you. And it will.

Don't joke: On finishing your drink at a local hostelry, 'Same again, please, landlord! Better get another one in before the whole place topples over the cliff. Ho ho!'

Heacham

Pocahontas

Heacham probably dates back several thousand years before Christ. It is famous now for its lavender fields which are known world-wide. The legend of Pocahontas, a Virginia Indian chief's daughter, was partly played out here also, with Pocahontas marrying John Rolfe in 1614. The Rolfes are buried in the village churchyard. Rolfe wrote that he loved Pocahontas but was also motivated by saving a heathen's soul by the marriage. They had a son called Thomas. At the end of her life she became very famous as she travelled around Britain, meeting James I amongst many other famous people, before she became ill and died in 1617. Films and books have added to the romantic story to the extent that fact is difficult to separate from fiction.

Lavender and luminous evening light

To see: This is the centre of the lavender growing industry and, in summer, the whole village smells lovely. You can visit a lavender farm and stock up on most welcome gifts for family and friends – everything from lavender soap to lavender plants for the garden.

Also to see: As the beach faces west and the sun sets over the immense sea, the most memorable and long-lingering sunsets occur, probably only rivalled by nearby Hunstanton. As a young boy, I remember a perfect summer's day would be, firstly, paying a visit to the old fashioned sweet and ice cream shop of two elderly brothers, Eric and John, in the village where we would have a drink of fizzy orangeade into which had been put a square of ice cream. The brothers would give us kids both a straw and a spoon and let us sit in the shop and devour this luscious concoction. Any excess change would be spent on blackjacks, fruit salads and pink sherbert flying saucers. Then, pockets bulging, we would wander up to the beach for a swim, ending the day bewitched by the orange, pink, silver and green 'highway of light' as the sun slowly – very, very, slowly – sank over the vast inland ocean. Summer days seemed so wonderfully long then!

The pebbly beach at Heacham.

Families flock to Hemsby beach on a hot summer's day.

Sand castles on the beach at Hemsby.

Hemsby

Hemsby dates back to Viking times. Today it is chiefly known for sandy beaches, ideal for a family day out. It used to have railway line – the Midland and Great Northern, known to the locals as the Muddle and Go Nowhere – but this closed in 1959. In Edwardian times, the engines had rich livery in black and orange, the coaches were matt brown, and the staff were very smart indeed. The trains may never have run at more than 25 mph in case they overran the upcoming station, but such a wonderfully dignified, beautiful and British enterprise must have been quite a sight to see.

To do: The sandy beaches are the greatest attraction and there are also many traditional seaside amusement arcades and cafes.

Heydon

Keeping it in the family

This tiny village with a population of under 100 in the 2001 census, five miles north of Reepham, is very special. It is only one of about a dozen villages in England in which everything – pub, houses, shops – is privately owned, in this case by the Bulwer Long family. It became Norfolk's first conservation area in 1971. You have to go out the same way you came in as there is no through road. It is well worth a visit, if only to see somewhere where there has been no new building for a hundred years. Hardly

Heydon is a small private village, historic and almost hidden thanks to its cul-de-sac style of entry and exit.

The pretty church of St Peter and St Paul in Heydon.

surprisingly, it has been the setting for some famous films, including L P Hartley's *The Go-Between* (see *Hunstanton*), William Makepeace Thackeray's *Vanity Fair* and Wilkie Collins' *The Woman in White*.

A footnote for folk who may like to own their own village: Most of those in the UK have been passed from generation to generation. Famous privately owned villages include Tissington in the Peak District and Clovelly in Devon. You'll need lots of money to mend all those roofs, fill in the potholes, fix the drains and maintain the cricket pavilion. They do just occasionally come onto the market: in 2009 Linkenholt in Hampshire reputedly changed hands for £25 million.

Holkham

Holkham can offer a small village, a lovely beach at Holkham Gap, and Holkham Hall, the home of the Earl of Leicester and Holkham, surrounded by a park with fallow deer. There is also a large wood of pine trees leading inland from the beach. The marshes are famous for their Pink-footed Geese.

Sadly, like in a lot of the coastal villages, the railway has closed, in this case in 1952. This has meant, however, that the area remains atmospheric and unspoilt which no doubt accounts for its popularity with film-makers. In 1976, parts of 'The Eagle has Landed' starring Sir Michael Caine, was made here. 'Shakespeare in Love' and more recently the very popular Norfolk-based TV drama 'Kingdom', starring one of the county's favourite sons, Stephen Fry, were partially filmed on the beach.

Holkham beach and sand dunes stretch for miles.

The Poppy Line steam train puffs from Sheringham to Holt stopping at Weybourne.

Holt

Holt is a very pretty Georgian town in the North Norfolk countryside, with a population of about 3500. It was largely rebuilt after a terrible fire in 1708 and today offers everything for a perfect weekend getaway: there are antique shops, arts and crafts exhibitions, lots of excellent places to have either afternoon tea or a sumptuous meal, and the beaches of the North Norfolk coast are only a short distance away.

To do: Wandering around the town is very nice. You will see some exceptionally fine Georgian houses, and also the Norman parish church of St Andrew which survived the great fire intact enough to be repaired. 'Blind Sam' is the name given to the Queen Victoria Jubilee Lantern, originally in the Market Place but relocated in 1921 to Obelisk Plain. The curious name is hardly a compliment as it refers to the frequent breakdown of the lantern in the early days which was because the local gas supply could, charitably, be called erratic. Note also the Obelisk, one of a pair originally made to serve as gateposts for Melton Constable Park. Dereham has the other – or, rather it doesn't any longer, not on show at any rate, as the locals threw it down a well at the beginning of World War II in order not to help the enemy, which is where it remains.

Leaves turn fiery red and orange as autumn reaches Holt.

Holt is noted for its Christmas lights which local people will tell you are the best in the county – the local economy receives a big boost at this time of year as the town is a quintessential Yuletide shopping venue. Stores include Bakers and Larners of Holt, East Anglia's answer to Fortnum & Mason, a fine establishment selling all sorts of things – great food, books and clothes amongst other products.

The town is also well-known for being taken over by Daleks every now and again in the incredibly popular Dr Who Festivals. A recent experiment has been a summer Arts Festival, the first of which was held for a week in 2009, and an initiative that will hopefully prove permanent.

A little way out of town is Holt Country Park, popular for family picnics, walking and orienteering. You can join one of the special 'mini beast' safaris – lots of fun for the little ones.

Also to do: An absolute 'must do' is to take a trip on the Poppy Line. A steam train will take you past poppy fields and some of the most beautiful scenery Norfolk has to offer, to Sheringham. This is an independent heritage railway.

The pretty Staithe and Willow Restaurant in Horning.

Horning

Horning is situated on the River Bure and we know that it dates back at least 1000 years, as records show that, in 1020, King Canute gave the manor to the Abbey of St Benet at Hulme.

Homes with scenic views along on the River Bure at Horning

NORFOLK

Horning is a popular stop for those cruising the Norfolk Broads.

It is an absolute gem of a village-on-the-water, although it can, not surprisingly, get busy in summer when the local population of just over 1000 is swelled by people from all over the world, attracted by the boats on hire, the scenery, local walking trails, trips up the river in a paddle steamer, good food and convivial pubs. There are also some great local shops and a 13th century church, St Benedict.

Horsey Dunes, sometimes called Horsey Gap

'When the tide comes in at the Horsey Gap
Without a previous warning,
A swan will build it's rushy nest
On the roof of the Swan at Horning.
And a balderheaded crow, contented and merry,
Shall feast on the corpses
That float by the ferry'

Old Horsey rhyme

Winter is a great time to see Grey Seals and pups on the beach.

This gruesome verse was no doubt based on facts as the land is flat and at the mercy of the sea – this would at times have been disastrous as Horsey Gap used to be the mouth of the River Thurne. The area was much loved by the presently underrated Victorian novelist (he is seen usually as just a master of melodrama, but I think this is unfair as did Dickens, so I am in good company), Wilkie Collins, who introduced the area in *Armadale* (1866). John Betjeman was another fan.

To see: Large colonies of butterflies, especially the Grayling and Dark Green Fritillary, are here. Grey Seals breed in winter. Close by is Horsey Windpump (1912). Open on certain days this five-storey mill gives fantastic views of Horsey Mere.

Star trails captured at Horsey Mill. The North Star (Polaris) is located in the centre of the trails. Although it appears the stars are moving it is, in fact, Earth's rotation that causes this effect. Photograph taken with kind permission from the National Trust, www.nationaltrust.org.uk

How Hill

This is a tiny – population only 54 in the 2001 census – but lovely centre for boating in the south of the county. There are lots of windmills, mostly for pumping water and drainage purposes. Do take a look, too, at the round tower of St Mary's Church – there are only a hundred and twenty-odd in the whole county.

To do: you can visit How Hill, built by Norwich's celebrated son, Edward Boardman, in 1904: it is run by the How Hill Trust.

Sunset at Turf Fen Mill, near Howe Hill – motionless and so peaceful.

Reflections on the River Ant at Howe Hill – a picture of pure tranquility.

Traditional reed cutting occurs at Howe Hill each winter.

Hunstanton

'The past is a foreign country; they do things differently there'
The Go-Between, L.P. Hartley

Let's build a new town

Quite a few places on the North Norfolk Coast received a huge boost from being 'discovered' in the 19th century: Hunstanton (pronounced 'Hunstan' just to catch out unsuspecting visitors) goes one step further as it was actually built from scratch at this time. True, there had been an 'old' Hunstanton since at least AD 500: Edmund, son of the King of Saxony, is said to have landed here at the age of 14 in 855 before being crowned King of East Anglia the following year. Subsequently defeated and taken prisoner by the invading Vikings, he was offered his life provided he gave up Christianity. He refused and was executed, later becoming the first patron saint of England.

It was in 1846, however, that Henry Styleman Le Strange persuaded a wealthy group of investors to build a 'new' Hunstanton a little way along the cliffs, together with a railway

The Wash at 'Sunny Hunny' provides some fantastic opportunities for wind surfers and kite surfing.

to King's Lynn. First, a lonely Royal Hotel was built but thereafter a whole town in shades of golden 'Honeystone'. It was and is beautiful, and the whole project a fantastic success.

Nature's unpredictable moods – the benign…
And what a place to build a new resort! From the top of the town the green slopes towards the sea over which the sun sets in spectacular fashion – Hunstanton is rare in facing west and the sun does actually set over the sea. For up to five or six hours a silver and golden, at times also pink and red, even greenish, 'roadway' – some locals call it the 'pathway to heaven' – stretches to infinity over the waves. When the tide recedes and it is peaceful, scores of seals bask on the sandbanks. This is also a place of mirages: magical ships and beautiful castles have been seen through the fine haze on a summer's day, on the horizon just above the sea.

…and the ferocious…
If there is a reasonable wind, there is no better place for windsurfing. Yet, when a gale blows and the sea roars, it is best to take cover – the pier was completely swept away in 1978. King John is reputed to have lost the Crown Jewels in the Wash due to a storm of unprecedented ferocity, so somewhere out there may be riches beyond imagination – tho' some historians think this may have been an early insurance scam, King John having secured the jewels somewhere else! Again, legend has it that when St Felix was sailing in the Wash on his way to bring Christianity to East Anglia in AD630, his boat became tossed in a storm. The resident beavers came to his rescue and, in gratitude, he granted the chief beaver Episcopal status before landing at nearby Babingley: this is why the first Bishop of Norfolk is reputed to have been a beaver.

It is hardly surprising that many writers have found inspiration here, including P G Woodhouse.

A cruel cut

One of the most celebrated novelists associated with Hunstan is L P Hartley. In 1944 he published *The Shrimp and the Anemone* which drew upon his childhood experiences playing among the rock pools below the famous cliffs. I became aware of him at university through the book *The Go-Between*, a work immeasurably melancholy and beautiful in almost equal proportions. I remember when the film, shot in Norfolk, came out because a fellow student, Nick, with whom I shared a house, returned from the long vacation to announce that he had been an extra in it and, furthermore, had been given a line: only three words – ' Is that so?' – but three words nonetheless. To 20 year old undergrads this was indeed something. When the film came to Canterbury about a dozen of us, with a beaming Nick in our rowdy midst, invaded the local cinema to see it. We were almost evicted due to our proud exhuberance. When we went home, though, it was in a very different and crushed frame of mind: Nick's sentence, and indeed any visual image of him, had been cut.

A ripping tale

The author spent many happy and exciting teenage years in 'Sunny Hunny', as we locals called it. We had a restaurant overlooking the green and pier. Providing food for visitors has always been a major part of the local economy.

My career as a businessman began and ended here in a very short time. What happened was that my Mum took on the restaurant with very little money: everything was repainted and repaired if possible. It had an outside patio upon which stood several old metal tables and wood-and-canvas chairs – all of which were, of course, repaired and put to use. It was a lovely spot to have afternoon tea. One day, a family, which included what Alexander McCall Smith in his fabulous *Ladies No.1 Detective Agency* series would have called a 'traditionally built lady', arrived and I, 13 years old and hanging outside trying-to-be-useful, directed them to a seat. Suddenly… 'RRRip…' The lady in question was on the concrete floor, the old canvas having ripped and the wooden arms of the erstwhile chair around her ample middle. 'Don't worry', I said, trying to disengage her from the vice-like wreckage. 'The chairs were old anyway!' Thank God she was so nice about it but, thereafter, I was banished to kitchen duties.

The promenade at Hunstanton features pretty gardens and leads to the famous cliffs and lighthouse.

Seaweed-capped boulders create a remarkable landscape on Hunstanton beach.

Doggie sense

The railway, alas, closed in 1969. My family remembers it well, though, as it was the means to many a happy or surprising excursion. One in particular comes to mind.

My sister, Juliet, was five years older than me and liked to go to dances and stuff. One day, she went down the green with her friend, Chrissie, to the station and took a train – alas, not now existing – to a local hop a couple of stops along the line.

Meanwhile, our family Labrador, Rum, was having none of it. He was a jealous dog. He jumped his chain and followed my sister.

My sister arrived at the hop and saw an attractive young man who introduced himself. 'Hello, I'm John'.

'I'm… I'm… Juliet' she began. At the same moment a beautiful Labrador bounded up to her and lay on his back, tail wagging furiously. ' And this is my dog, Rum.'

It emerged afterwards that Rum had got on the train, sniffed in every carriage and got off at the same stop as Juliet. Scent or sense?

To eat

The inland side of the town grows rather a lot of fine potatoes and, with the Wash the other side, fish and chips are justly famous. The dish became a staple of the poorer classes around the middle of the 19th century but is now regarded, at best, as quintessential fine English fair. Hunstan's are the best. At the time of writing, the *Eastern Daily Press* reports that one chap regularly takes a round trip of 7 hours in order to buy his meal here and nowhere else.

To do

You can walk along the top of the cliffs past St Edmund's Church and the lighthouse or along the beach which is better to see the red chalk limestone and white chalk layers, as well as enjoying the fresh water pools and tiny crabs all around you. The Wash as a whole is famous for shrimps, cockles and mussels.

To watch

This area is also a favourite spot for migrating geese, ducks and wading birds. A recent report suggests that two million birds (I wonder how they count them? '…39, 40,41, stay still will you, you swirling roost! Oh, I've lost count again!') use the area for roosting and feeding: some are partial to shellfish. There are also Curlews, Redshanks, Lapwings and Grey and Golden Plovers to name but some – a visual feast for the bird-lover.

You can also wander around and look at this remarkable town, bearing in mind its recent birth. There are the usual arcades and so on, and a long and lovely prom.

Don't say

In the local fishmonger: 'Have you got any fresh shrimps from Billingsgate?'

The striking red and white chalk cliffs at Hunstanton are rich in fossils.

Ingoldisthorpe

I used to go to school here. We were transported from our boarding house at nearby Heacham in an arthritic old double decker bus that daily threatened to stop and go backwards as it wheezed and shook its way up the steep hill that leads to the church: it always just managed it, though, which was a tad disappointing to eight and nine year old schoolboys.

Bits and pieces of history
Pronounced 'Inglesthorpe', this very pretty place dates back at least two thousand years – a complete Roman skeleton was found some years ago. We also know some bits and pieces of its history: in 850 the Lord of the Manor was called Ingulf; and in the 13th century Thomas de Ingoldisthorpe was convicted of the murder of his brother, Drugo, and part of his sentence was to find and pay for a priest to pray for Drugo's soul for seven years. Better records were kept in more recent times and we know that the handsome rectory was built in 1858 when it had a yearly rent-tithe of £312 and the village population stood at 309. Many times I scurried, partly in awe and partly in fear as us little ones found the atmosphere a little daunting, to and from the Perpendicular church of St Michael to sing in the choir. This was substantially restored at the same time as the rector gained his fine home.

A ghost
The rector's fine house was, in fact, the schoolhouse, later in its life, that I attended as a very young nipper along with my bro' and sis'. It held a terror. On the first floor at the

The handsome church of St Michael at Ingoldisthorpe.

top of the main and very grand staircase was a further small set of stairs. This led into a small room with a very high ceiling, across the top of which ran a stout oak beam. In the middle of the room was a very beautiful blue and white Victorian toilet. No one used it, though, as rumour had it that a maid to the original vicar, abandoned by her lover, had hanged herself from the beam. Many and many a time, heart pounding and eyes averted, I and my little colleagues rushed past that fearful spot. We never did see her. However, I recently went back to the house and was lucky enough to meet one of the residents – it has been converted into spacious flats now. I asked the lady if my memory was just a childhood fantasy. 'No,' she remarked, 'she is still here. Nobody has seen her but, sometimes, especially when it is stormy, you can hear her crying out'.

Two famous ladies
The village sign has a tale to tell for it depicts two famous ladies of the village. On one side is Agnes Bigge who died in 1608 and her legacy of £10, having been wisely invested and managed over the centuries, still manages to provide Christmas treats for the elderly and poor. On the other side is Mrs Tylden, a formidable lady by all accounts, who became Lady of the Manor in 1909, lived to be over 100, and knew Queen Alexandra intimately. She wrote of being most gratified by the respect shown by common people as she drove around in her carriage. To us schoolboys, she was a mythical figure, and a common piece of advice to a newly arrived five year old was ' Behave yourself or Mrs Tylden will get you'. Going outside on your own after dark was completely out of the question.

King's Lynn

'On the Borders of that mysterious and dangerous arm of the German Ocean, called 'The Wash', and swept by the chilly blasts that come roaring and raging away from the distant ice fields of the north, and sometimes enveloped in the salt sea fogs that creep up over the flats of the marshland, and enfold in their embrace its shipping and houses, stands the quaint, historic, interesting town of Lynn Regis'.
Rev W. B. Russell Caley, M.A., F.R.H.S., writing in Bygone Norfolk,
(William Andrews and Co, London, 1898)

'Bob of Lynn during Twenty long Years,
Directed, perplex'd and mismanag'd affairs:
A Whig out of Place, and a Tory when in;
And a very great Trimmer was Bob of Lynn'.

Contemporary verse on Sir Robert Walpole, MP for King's Lynn – earlier he was elected MP for the rotten borough of Castle Rising – and the country's first Prime Minister 1721-42.

Once a thriving port, there are still fishing boats and trawlers to be found moored on the quay at King's Lynn, waiting for the incoming tide on the Great River Ouse.

'There was a young lady of Lynn
Who was deep in original sin.
When they said 'Do be good!'
She said 'Would if I could!'
And straightway went at it again.'

Anonymous

Changes

In his beautifully written and entertaining book *The Companion Guide to East Anglia* (Collins: 1971), John Seymour writes 'The most romantic town in East Anglia is King's Lynn'. I well remember this as being true as I had recently finished a happy seven-year secondary education there. It may have been a bit down-at-heel, yes, but the overwhelming majority of the medieval buildings remained and the town had a mellow 'aura'. Regrettably, the 'decade that good taste forgot' followed, which affected the whole

Huge anchors in Purfleet Quay lie close to the magnificent Customs House (1684).

King's Lynn Town Hall dates from 1423 and has been much modified inside and out. It has served as a prison, a house of correction, a courtroom, council chambers and as an assembly room for state functions. The cells were in use until 1937.

of UK life: in architecture, insensitive concrete monoliths came into vogue; men wore shoes with gold chains on them, flared jeans, and kipper ties with red and green flowers all over; kitchens were decorated with brown walls and orange ceilings (my brother did this, to his great delight, in our kitchen) and people hankered after an avocado green bathroom suite (they always looked dirty so there was little point in cleaning them). King's Lynn – or Bishop's Lynn, Lynn Regis or simply, Lynn, suffered greatly at this period as did my home city of Norwich. How better things would have been had we had a moratorium on any new developments from 1970 to 1990, or even a little later.

For Lynn didn't deserve this. Following the establishment of the gorgeous St Margaret's Church in 1101 as part of his act of penance to the Pope for the act of 'simony' – having bought the right to be Bishop of Norwich for the huge sum of nineteen hundred pounds – by Herbert de Losinga, King's Lynn rose to become one of the largest ports in the Kingdom. The Customs House (1684) and many other fine buildings resulted and, with a bit of a wobble until the railways once again brought prosperity after 1847, the town did pretty well. A second renaissance followed with the arrival of Campbell's Soups in

1958. At the time of writing, a great debate is on about what to do with the original Campbell's factory – a building so uncompromising that it has a defiant beauty to it. Much remains to be done. A multi-million pound redevelopment of the town centre is underway which will include extensive cycle lanes – seven times as many people than the national average travel to work each day by bike. The future of this ancient town is in the balance.

A place of learning… and murder

Lynn has always been a centre of learning. The most famous person to go to school here was Princess Diana. There has been a grammar school of sorts for many hundreds of years, until recently when King Edward VII Grammar, which I attended, became a Sports College. However, attending the school gave me knowledge of one of the town's most notorious people – a master at the school.

He was apparently a very learned man who was, alas, hanged for murder in 1759. His name was Eugene Aram and, to this day, debate continues as to whether or not he was guilty. Sir Edward Bulwer-Lytton wrote a famous novel about him in 1832 and he became a Victorian cause célèbre. He was accused of murdering one, Daniel Clark, who may or may not have been having an affair with his wife, and with whom he was involved in a tawdry affair to do with stolen silver plate. In court he represented himself very eloquently, though evidently not eloquently enough, and many were the King Edward VII schoolboys who took up his cause in a re-enactment of the complex case. The proceedings would generally peak with an emotional recitation of his last written words in the early hours of the morning on which he was hanged (he tells us that it was after 3am because he had slept soundly until that hour):

> *Come, pleasing rest! Eternal slumbers fall!*
> *Seal mine, that once must seal the eyes of all.*
> *Calm and composed my soul her journey takes;*
> *No guilt that troubles, and no heart that aches.*
> *Adieu, thou sun! All bright, like her, arise!*
> *Adieu, fair friends, and all that's good and wise!*

Execution most gruesome: a fact of life in medieval times.

In the book, *Discover Norwich* (Halsgrove 2009), I remark that my home city of Norwich has had, overall, a peaceful history but that the few examples of bloodletting have been particularly gruesome. This was referring to, firstly, the burning alive of ordinary folk in the name of religion, at Lollard's Pit down by the river, a few hundred yards from the present station. It also refers to the punishments meted out to Kett's flock after their unsuccessful rebellion in 1549. Those that were hanged had the easiest death. Hundreds

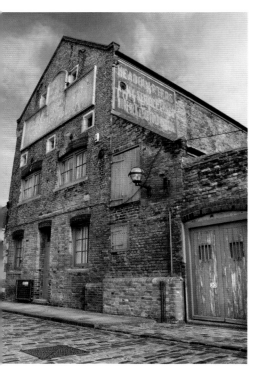

In Purfleet Quay, King's Lynn, this wonderful old building was once the Headquarters for the Army Service Corp, Norfolk and Suffolk Brigade.

more were hanged, drawn and quartered in the market place, a death so terrible that it must have provided the 'inspiration' for the disposal of the corrupt police chief in the Hannibal Lecter film. Others were laid on the ground and tied to a horse which galloped away over the cobbles and, well, yes....

I thought, as a historian of these things, I was quite hardened until I researched the following method of capital punishment practised in Norfolk, with the fine town of King's Lynn giving it an unspeakable twist. A cauldron of water would be set up and a fire lighted underneath. When it was boiling, the felon would be dropped in. In 1531 in

The Corn Exchange in King's Lynn plays home to many shows and events.

Lynn, however, this was indeed done but, in addition, a gibbet with chain was placed above the cauldron. A girl servant, convicted of poisoning her mistress, was attached to the end of the chain and lowered in, then raised, then lowered again until her screams ceased. Executions were very big business right up to Victorian times, with crowds feasting, drinking, buying 'confessions' ostensibly written by the deceased, and holding a series of entertainments afterwards. Folklore suggested that women who could not conceive would have more luck in the future if they could 'touch' the body of an executed person, so bribery of those conducting the executions was rife.

I have not come across any more examples of this method of execution and of that I am very glad.

An important point is that, in our region, life in medieval times was seen as a bonus, about as secure as a spider in the bathtub. We had the plague, tuberculosis, cholera, poisoning – by food and alcohol – starvation, and no knowledge of the basics of good health. To survive for a week or even a day was a major cause of celebration and, if someone else was gone, Phew! At least you were left. The insignificance of life is apparent in this traditional rhyme:

> *He enjoyed himself while he was here*
> *Went on the same from year to year*
> *But where he's gone and how he fare*
> *Nobody knows and nobody care.*

To do: As befits such a major town, there is always much going on. There are two festivals each year – one of classical music (King's Lynn Festival) whilst the other one (Festival Too) is one of the largest free music festivals in Europe, attracting top stars.

Each year, on Valentine's Day, a travelling funfair called The Mart sets up in Tuesday Market Place for a fortnight.

There is The Walks if you wish to stroll in a beautiful 18th century park. It is grade II listed.

Be sensitive when discussing: Football. I fondly remember the thrill of bunking off Saturday afternoon activities in my boarding house to go see our local team. We would have a fizzy drink and a luke-warm square slab of pastry containing a strange brown goo that was called a ' meat pie'. Unfortunately, King's Lynn football team – The Linnets – was wound up in the High Court at the end of 2009.

Morston

Just about a mile from Blakeney, Morston was also once a very important port. It is beautiful seal-watching country. Boat trips can be taken from Morston Quay.

Morning reflections in Morston Harbour.

Families prepare their boats for a fun day of sailing at Morston.

Muckleburgh Collection

This museum is located on the site of the former Weybourne Camp (see section on Weybourne), which was used for gunnery practice until 1960. In 1988 it was opened to the public with a limited collection of vehicles and a small museum detailing the camp's history. It has grown immensely since and is now a very popular day out for military enthusiasts and the general public. You can see many impressive military vehicles, guns and weapons, including an amphibious jeep, a Chieftain and a Scorpion tank, a bridgelayer, and some heavy artillery. There is also a stock of 2500 military uniforms. Mid 2010, Sir Michael Savory, owner and co-founder, announced a major revamp of the facilities to include a restaurant, lecture room and toilets (until now, along with everything else, of 1940s vintage!). Original features of the camp, including gun emplacements, will also be rebuilt.

Mundesley – incorporating the Church of St Peter, Knapton

'There is a grandeur about the cliffs and the sea foaming and tossing at their base from here to Cromer that no other part of the East Anglian coast possesses. And here at Mundesley the waves positively thunder upon the shore, lashing and plunging up these gigantic cliffs, and tearing away huge masses of earth as they recede; yet, when like a tired giant, the sea lies along the miles of firm white sands stretching right from Bacton to Sheringham, these shores make the grandest possible playground for the little ones and the most glorious promenade imaginable.'

Photo Pictures In East Anglia by Payne Jennings, Art Photo Works, Ashtead, Surrey. Undated work, possibly early 20th century

'Here lies Fred, who was alive, and is dead.
Had it been his father, I had much rather:
Had it been his mother, better than another:
Had it been his sister, no one would have missed her:
Had it been his entire generation,
So much better for the nation:
But since 'tis Fred, who was alive, and is dead,
There's no more to be said.'

Epitaph in St Botolph's Church, Trunch, about a mile inland from Mundesley (from East Anglian Epitaphs, R. Lamont-Brown, Acorn Editions 1981)

What's in a name?
Mundesley appeared in the Domesday Book of 1086 when it was variously known as 'Muselai' or 'Muleslai'. The name is likely to derive from the fact that the village of Mundesley is the final outlet point for the river *Mun*. Therefore the name of the river is conjoined with the word *leah*, which itself usually means *a clearing* or *open ground*.

The Ship Inn at Mundesley offers great food, refreshing ales and fine sea views.

The village today

The population of the village has grown very slowly since its first formation as a very small cluster of dwellings, likely to have been only single storey simple huts. In the 14th century there were less than 20 dwellings. By the 1841 census, the population had reached 455.

The coming and going of the railways

However, things were set to radically change when the railway arrived in Mundesley on 1 July 1898. The stylish station was designed and built with no less than three 600ft platforms. That's a lot for a small town. In the initial years the station saw sixteen trains arrive from North Walsham and beyond every day. In 1903 the large sum of £93,000 was invested in extending the line from Mundesley to Cromer but fifty years later the line was closed. Dr Beeching ended the railway altogether. Part of the old rail track route is now a delightful public walking area, known as Pigney's Wood.

A grand and golden age

Present day Mundesley has a population of approximately 2,700. In its late 19th century heyday Mundesley, like its neighbour Cromer, became such a fashionable summer coastal resort that no less than three new hotels were built to accommodate everyone. The Clarence opened in 1891 and The Grand and The Manor hotels took their first guests in 1897. Prior to this there was only one hotel, The Royal, which is an ancient building with its origins probably dating back to the early 17th century.

A roof of angels

We have already mentioned Knapton, and a treasure awaits here in the parish church of

Snow on the beach at Mundesley. Pink clouds glow in the setting sun.

St. Peter. On entering, look up and there above you, on well over 100 pairs of angels' wings, hovers the most amazingly carved roof of any church in Norfolk and, arguably, it's the finest in the land. John Smithe gifted this gloriously crafted creation to the church in 1503. It has been said that, on occasion, even the carved wooden eagle's head on the reader's lectern standing in the nave cannot resist twisting its neck up to look in admiration at the beauty above it.

Mundesley and the sea: The Jonet *story*
As is the case with all communities on the North Norfolk Coast, the immeasurable and unforgiving ocean has played a starring role in Mundesley history. One particular episode concerned the Dutch coaster vessel *Jonet*, which ran aground in a storm on Saturday 15 March 1969. She was thrown up on the beach and seriously damaged on a groin. As she was carrying at least 150 gallons of diesel, it was decided she would be set on fire to burn away the fuel so as to avoid any risk of pollution to the precious golden sands and its inevitable damage to wildlife and plants along the coast. A very popular café and restaurant on Beach Road is named after the ill-fated boat.

Lifeboats and Mundesley's 'never give up' British spirit
Mundesley has an in-shore lifeboat manned entirely by about twelve volunteers, including crew and back-up technicians. These admirable stalwarts are supported solely by public contributions and the brave service they provide is run quite independently from the Royal National Lifeboat Institute.

The grassy cliffs and pebbly beach at Mundesley disappear into the misty horizon.

The spirit of local unity is also very prevalent amongst a team of local folk who man the 24/7 coastal watch service. In the early 1990s, as part of the government's desire to scale down the national coast-watching service, the station at Mundesley was closed . However, the locals gained the ill-fated watch station a remarkable reprieve. It is now run quite independently of any of the previous central controls, by good-hearted local people.

Royal recognition
For this considerable achievement in providing a free and constant look-out facility, Her Majesty presented the local stalwarts with the '*Queen's Award for Voluntary Service*', in June 2009. And well deserved too.

To walk: Around the old defences
Take the short walk down the lane at the right hand side of the old Continental and head with care towards the sea and the cliff top. When the reverse of the old hotel is revealed on your left, turn immediately to your right. Here you will find part of the fortified defence system mainly built to protect this shoreline from enemy invasion during the Second World War. A battery of six-inch guns was installed here and the impressive foundations are still extant. You can climb up to precisely where the gun was mounted. You may find this site is strangely unnerving in its almost sinister silence. You are standing on an edifice of another age, which every year slips away yet further from common knowledge and memory. Just as you are left in wonder and perhaps awe of this massive structure, a small bird is very likely to suddenly appear from this bramble-strewn fortress to tell you that this place of previous last resort defence, is now its home, and you are the invader. Carefully retrace your steps back to the pathway and find the sloping walk in front of this structure. Following this you will find yourself on the beach below in fairly short time via a steeply angled path.

The anti-tank defence work here still looks formidable. If you follow this defensive work towards the village you will soon find easy stepped access to the sea-front promenade and the slope which eventually takes you back up to Beach Road.

Also too walk: The corn mills walk
Mundesley used to have two working corn mills. The main structure of Stow Mill, at Paston, is still extant but now converted into a private dwelling. It is well worth the half mile walk south along the B1159 to see it. The records suggest that this corn windmill was built ca.1827 and was a working mill for over one hundred years, closing for business in 1930. It is open to the public.

A disastrous fire in November 1956 destroyed the other mill, which was situated in the village itself. This watermill was believed to date back to 1723. It was unique in that it

Mundesley from a high vantage point along the cliff tops.

worked on the over-shot principle, where the water (falling from the large pond above the mill wheel), was projected at velocity on to the top paddles of the wheel. To get an unobstructed bird's eye view of the old millwheel it is necessary to take the public footpath from Paston Road (which leads to the pond) and, after only ten yards or so from the road, take a careful excursion to the left of the path to the wheel's brick-built pit. A cautionary look over the retaining wall will reveal the metal wheel and its spindle way down below you. Local belief is that upwards of 8 million gallons of water flowed through the mill every day, when it was working. It was rigged to generate electricity as well as grind corn.

It's a real joy to get this close to a bit of old industrial engineering. By rejoining the path and turning left you will soon discover the mill's large pond - complete with its quacking resident ducks.

To see: The Church of All Saints
Do go see the parish church of All Saints to the north of the village. A church, standing within twelve acres of land, is mentioned in the Domesday Book of 1086. The structure

of the present church is mainly of late 14th century date. In 1844, after years of neglect, it was decided to increase the size of the building, and an extension was built at the west end of the nave and a gallery inserted, which survives today. In 1903 the church was further extended and further work was completed in 1914. One fascinating memorial in the church on the north wall of the nave may well catch your eye. It records that it is in memory of *'Haringay residents who died in Clarence House 1941-1987'*. With no further explanation being available can we conjecture on these people being Second World War evacuees from London, who did not return home? Fascinating.

Also to see: A small but perfectly formed museum, and a memorial to the bravest of the brave. Mundesley can arguably claim to have one of the smallest museums in the world. It is housed in the ground floor area of what was the old coastguard lookout room, perched near the cliff top, on the pretty lawned area on Beach Road. It is certainly worth a visit.

The Mundesley Maritime Museum is also a coastwatch lookout.

Beach huts on Mundesley beach.

Norwich

'The inhabitants in general are remarked for their urbanity, hospitality, and the readiness with which they contribute to all public and private charitable institutions, the better classes for their taste and munificence; and greatly to the credit of the lower classes, much less of that inclination to dissoluteness of manners prevails among them than is usually found in large and populous cities. So strict is the attention of the magistrates, in checking of its earliest existence the progress of vice and immorality, that the execution of a criminal in the city does not occur for many years together...'

Assessment of the Norwich character in *The History of Norwich from the Earliest Records to the Present Time* by P. Browne. Printed and sold by Bacon, Kinnebrook, & Co. Undated publication but probably about 1815.

There is nowhere you can go in this ancient medieval city that is not interesting. The 'centre of gravity' has shifted from time to time but every part, almost every street, has had its moment in the sun, historically speaking.

Centre of gravity shifts over the ages
Coslany was the first part of town to be occupied in Saxon times. Later, 'Norwich yards' took hold here. These 'yards' consisted of a number of two roomed houses with a

A wide vista of the Norwich skyline, showing the Castle, St Peter Mancroft, The Forum, City Hall and both Cathedrals: A fine City indeed!

bathhouse and toilet at the end nearest the river. The river was used for all purposes – drinking, dying cloth and disposing of human and other waste. Disease was rife and poverty dreadful. Folk would make their own beer, or buy a barrel from one of the many breweries in this area, and sell the often dubious cocktail to neighbours. The chief recreation for many was either drinking or building a church: many families worked, generation after generation on a particular house of God. As late as 1925, records show that the authorities wanted to pull down 3000 dwellings that were unfit for human habitation here. Today, all has been reversed as this is an affluent and very pleasant area in which to live with an easy to walk to and from the City centre.

Norwich drinking in general
It is worth bearing in mind that, despite what our present tabloids would suggest, drinking has been going on to excess for probably as long as man has existed. This was not just a way of life for the 'common man' – it also extended very much to 'higher' society, where port and strong liquor were thought to enliven the blood and refresh the mind. Some doctors would prescribe brandy or champagne to their patients when all else had failed, a few well-known 18th and 19th century figures reputedly having had a last drinking bout before meeting their maker. Gout was known as a wealthy man's ailment (it was brought on by too much fortified wine) and people were by no means always ashamed of it. And Norwich has for centuries been famous for its fine quality brews. In the most entertaining small book *East Anglian Reminiscences*, edited by EA Goodwyn and JC Baxter (Boydell Press 1976), is an example of a song to be enjoyed when a goodly quantity of punch has flowed:

> *The man that takes nothing,*
> *And goes to bed sober,*
> *Dies as the leaves die, dies as the leaves die*
> *Dies as the leaves die,*
> *In the month of October.*
>
> *Let each man take his glass tonight,*
> *And go to bed mellow,*
> *And live as he ought to live, live as he ought to live,*
> *Live as he ought to live.*
> *And die a hearty fellow.*

The Conquest, Cathedral and Castle
Following the Norman Conquest, Herbert de Losinga was required by the Pope, as an act of penance for the serious moral crime of 'buying' the Bishopric of Thetford – he paid nineteen hundred pounds, a colossal sum – to build a Cathedral adjacent to Tombland.

Norwich Cathedral, one of the finest architectural and spiritual treasures of Europe.

He also built a Benedictine Monastery here. The first stone was laid by him in 1094. Tombland, which has nothing to do with 'tombs' but derives from the Norse word 'thum' meaning 'empty space', became the new centre of the city with a thriving market. The soaring proportions of the Cathedral Church of the Holy and Undivided Trinity, with its thousand roof bosses and compelling pristine spirit, has remained the chief glory of this city, even though the 'busyness' of life is best manifested nowadays in other parts. Her Majesty Queen Elizabeth II is, at the very moment of writing, opening the new Hostry, the largest building project in the Cathedral's history since its inception. It has been eleven years in the making, and is designed by Sir Michael Hopkins.

The nearby Castle was also built at this time. The Normans wanted to impose their authority on those who may be tempted to oppose them. It is a fine structure, of Caen stone, resurfaced in Victorian times. Robert Kett was hanged in chains over the walls following his rebellion in 1549. Yet, it never had a monarch live here. It has a fascinating museum inside, which includes a 19th century bird collection, a wonderful array of paintings by the 'Norwich School' – notably John Crome and John Sell Cotman – and a

The magnificent Norwich Castle in winter.

The Cathedral Church of the Holy and Undivided Trinity, warmed by the rising sun on a winter's morning.

world-beating display of ceramic teapots. The most memorable exhibits for me, however, are the death masks of felons who were hanged just outside: many believed that criminal tendencies could be seen by the shape of the head but, to the untrained eye, apart the imprint of the death rope, these specimens have little in common.

King Street, just down from the Castle was, during this period, the most important street in the city. Slightly later, Elm Hill – at the other end of Tombland - became fashionable. It was the home of many prosperous merchants and civic personalities, including the Paston family who bequeathed us the Paston Letters, which is still in print. Thereafter, Elm Hill fell into decay and was only saved from destruction in the early 20th century by a single vote of the Council.

Down by the River
During the First World War, the Riverside area – down by the station – gained great importance as it was the home of Boulton & Paul, a famous Norwich firm capable of producing just about anything in metal. During the conflict, they produced more of the famous Sopwith Camel aircraft than anyone else: these were tested out on Mousehold Heath . The site of the main factory – now a block of modern luxury flats – is named after another of their aircraft, the Sidestrand bomber. At the time of their greatest success, another legendary Norwich firm – Jeremiah Colman (of mustard fame) – was situated just up the river. Both firms have 'gone' now, Boulton & Paul to Wolverhampton while Colman's mustard is part of Unilever. The 'Riverside Quarter' is now the new entertainment centre of the city with fine modern flats, nightclubs, restaurants and a multiplex cinema.

Put on your boots
Another vital aid to the First World War effort was the Norwich boot, made over the other side of town, mainly. Here is a celebration of this industry, as recorded in *The Peace Souvenir, Norwich War Record*. Edited by Herbert Leeds, Jarrold & Sons 1919:

'Whatever criticisms may be levelled against Britishers regarding the conduct of the war and the supply of materials of war, nothing but praise is due to the excellence of the British marching boot. Friend and foe alike have testified in no ungrudging way to the supremacy of the footwear supplied to our troops as compared with the productions of other countries, and it would be difficult to imagine a better testimony than is provided by the fact of the wonderful organisation created by the Germans to secure by hook or by crook every available pair of British boots – an operation in which respect was paid neither to the living or the dead.

That Norwich played an important part in equipping our men and those of our Allies with large quantities of boots and shoes is a matter for the greatest congratulation.'

The final resting place for members of the Colman (of Mustard fame) family
(Photographed by Stephen Browning).

Dark days, bright humour

The terrible suffering of the First World War was alleviated to a degree by the humour of the people of the city. Indeed, the pain was scarcely known as the government kept the lid on the true scale of incompetence and disaster that preceded victory. It only became clear many years later. My own Dad was one of the few survivors of the Somme: he was 19 years old and he could never find words to begin to describe what he had seen. We kids knew better than to ask him about it. Anyway, people continued to see the funny side and here is a description of life in a blackout.

Norwich during the blackout – 1915

On nights of extreme darkness the conditions were not without a comic aspect. Sober and respected citizens were unable to find their own homes, or feeling sure that they could not be mistaken, boldly walked into somebody else's house. Ladies who took two or three turns in by-streets, lost their bearings, and had to enquire of passers-by where they were. Pedestrians walked into trees, lamp-posts, street orderly bins, any obstruction in the highway, sometimes with serious results to themselves. Nervous people of both sexes shrieked out every time they heard footsteps, and thoughtless people did much execution with umbrella-ribs. Some protected themselves from collisions with a luminous disc pinned to their clothing in some prominent position. Never was there so little traffic in Norwich streets after nightfall.

Peace Souvenir, Norwich War Record. Edited by Herbert Leeds, Jarrold & Sons 1919

A fine market for a Fine City

Today, for most people going about their everyday business, the centre of town is the Market Place. This has been the 'social' hub of Norwich since, probably, the 18th Century. At the bottom of the square is the wonderfully named Gentleman's Walk. The male of the species was, in olden days, the 'Peacock'. Dressed in silk waistcoats, with wigs suitably powdered, gentlemen would try to attract the ladies and also celebrate the fact that they were masters of the universe by parading up and down Gentleman's Walk, dropping into the many coffee houses for a chat with their peers. It is interesting that the term 'Tuck Shop' – evidenced in public schools all over the Empire – may have originated from 'Tuck's Coffee House' which was an attraction here. It had a library of sorts and the latest papers, along with sweets and delicacies to be enjoyed.

The Market Place has recently been revamped and all stalls replaced in line with current trading laws. The vibrant coloured tops of the units have been retained. It is always changing as it is a crucible of modern retail ideas: thus we have a unit trading in Polish food, another in fine coffees, one specialising in Norfolk cheese and ice cream, and look - here's one that sells strawberry and avocado soap! It is great place to propose a new business without the crippling overheads of a shop in an established street – and Norwich people are very enterprising. Thus, if you want to see the next 'big thing', you can do worse than wander about this market.

Statue of The Duke of Wellington, victor of Waterloo and adopted son of Norwich, in the ancient grounds at Norwich Cathedral
(Photographed by Stephen Browning).

Christmas lights sparkle in the Market Place.

Pigeons and chips

The area in front of the Forum – ie above the Market Place – has lately been redesigned as a modern version of a small Greek amphitheatre. There are bands here; and all sorts of exhibitions. At Christmas time an ice-rink has proved popular, and of course there is a tree. Sitting and standing on the steps will be citizens eating and drinking, mostly food from the market: I have never seen so many discarded chips fed upon by voracious pigeons – if pigeons could text each other, they would surely all congregate here and Norwich would likely become the scene from Hitchcock's 'The Birds – the Revenge'.

Here is how it appeared two hundred years ago:

The marketplace about 1815

The centre of the market is appropriated to persons from the country, who, on market days, sit here with stalls, hampers, and pads, for the sale of butter, cheese, eggs, poultry, and butcher's meat; there are three large pairs of scales, with weights provided by the committee, which all persons may freely use; and there is no toll demanded for any of the before-mentioned articles. The East side of the Market-place is for the sale of garden stuff, the North end for fish, and the South end is the fruit market. Herbage and fruit pay a small toll collected by the clerk of the market; these last articles are sold here every day of the week, and on Sundays all stalls, etc, are taken away. The Upper Market is situated on the West side of the Great Market, near the North entrance of St Peter's church, to the West of which is the Butchery and the Shambles, between which lies the Fish-market.

Assessment of the Norwich character in *The History of Norwich from the Earliest Records to The Present Time* by P. Browne. As above

Just below the Forum, in Haymarket, is a statue of Sir Thomas Browne , one of the most influential gentlemen in Norwich's history. He wrote *Religio Medici*, a work of international renown concerning the raison d'etre of the medical profession. He was knighted by Charles II in 1671. We have this description of the event:

Knighthood of Sir Thomas Browne
1671. His majesty king Charles the Second, with the queen, and the dukes of York, Monmouth and Buckingham, visited this city. They kept their court at the duke's palace, in Maddermarket, and were magnificently entertained by Lord Henry Howard, afterwards Duke of Norfolk. His majesty attended divine service at the cathedral, visited the bishop at his palace, and afterwards came to guildhall, and shewed himself to his subjects from the balcony, and dined with the corporation at a sumptuous dinner provided at the new hall …. After dinner his majesty conferred the honour of knighthood on Dr Thomas Browne, one of the most learned and worthy persons of the age. The mayor, Thomas Thacker esq declined that honour.

The last sentence is intriguing.

Assessment of the Norwich character in *The History of Norwich from the Earliest Records to The Present Time* by P. Browne. As above

Character of Sir Thomas Browne
From the same source we learn :

He was a person of most extensive learning and profound judgement; very eminent in his medical profession, and of extensive practice: he was a sincere professor of the religion of the church of England, which he dignified by his unaffected piety, strict morality, unbounded charity, and benevolence: his probity rendered him universally respected, and his benevolence generally beloved: in his person he was comely and venerable, as appears from his picture, which hangs in the vestry of St Peter's Mancroft church.

Note: The picture is still there.

Norwich – the most learned city in the land
Norwich was the first provincial city in the country to have a library – from 1608. Of course, access was restricted to the upper echelons of society as many believed that knowledge, given freely to the lower orders, would only breed discontent. The common

Statue of Sir Thomas Browne on Hay Hill, Norwich
(Photographed by Stephen Browning).

St Peter Mancroft, mistaken by some for the Anglican Cathedral itself. John Wesley, who knew about these things, said he had never seen a more beautiful parish church.

man was designed by God to 'go up one furrow and down another'. To show him a better life was unkind and he would inevitably become unhinged. This feeling was regarded as proved by the French Revolution next century.

A more formal library was set up in 1784. Here is an account of this library written about 1815. The fees would have been out of the question for all but the wealthy:

A very neat building, formerly a chapel for the Roman Catholic religion, under the patronage of the Duke of Norfolk. When the chapel in St John's churchyard was erected, this building was lease of the duke, for the purpose to which it is now applied, and for which it is very convenient. In October, 1794, the library was removed hither from the city library-room, in St Andrew's hall, where it had been kept from the time of its first institution in 1784. The terms of admission are two guineas and a half; after which the subscription is only twelve shillings annually. The collection of books consists of upwards of

6000 volumes, and are increasing. There are at present more than 500 subscribers, twenty-four of whom constitute a committee, exclusive of the president, vice-president, and ex-president. Twelve of the committee are chosen annually, and each member sits two years. The librarian takes care of and delivers out the book every day between the hours of eleven and two, and seven and nine in the evening from the 1st of September to the last day in April, Sundays and some particular festivals excepted.

Assessment of the Norwich character in *The History of Norwich from the Earliest Records to The Present Time* by P. Browne. As above.

Thus, until well into the last century, it was seen as a great privilege to be allowed to take out books. There were lots of rules and regulations – no pencil marks, no turning down of pages, no exposure of the books to wind and rain etc. During research in the Reserve Section of the present library, I came across a library book dated 1898 which, at the end of a long list of *do's* and *don'ts*, had this rather alarming statement: '*INFECTIOUS DISEASES. Readers in whose homes there occurs any case of infectious disease must deliver all Library books in their keeping to the medical officer of the Borough and make no further use of the library until the house has been declared free from infection.*' It was thought that cholera could possibly be spread by books.

Today, The Millennium Library at the top of the Market Place is a very fine structure, horse-shoe shaped, designed by Sir Michael Hopkins and built of hand-made bricks. As well as books, you can have a pizza or beer here, take out CDs and films or research your family history. It is very friendly with helpful staff but it can be noisy – the building as a whole is called 'The Forum', which means 'meeting place' in Latin, which is just how many citizens use it. Proud to relate, it is the most successful library complex in the country which is as it should be, Norwich having pioneered a 'book-lending' service more than four hundred years ago.

For more serious study, in perfect peace overlooking The Broad, you can go to the UEA Library – day passes are available upon proof of address and photographic ID. Books can be consulted for reference purposes. There are Libraries and there are Libraries. This is the latter. World class, as you might expect.

The beautiful game
The local football team is called 'The Canaries' and this region is football mad. Former football songs were not perhaps as catchy as they are today but they had a romance about them: this is part of the Canaries' song in the early days (Norwich Football Club came into being in 1902):

> *'To our Norwich City we mean to bring fame;*
> *With our Norwich City we'll play such a game*

That Fulham and Tottenham will faint at the name
Of Norwich Canaries, what-ho!'

That football in this area has long been the subject of passion is evident by the following quote. It is from Sir Thomas Elyot and dates from the 16th century:

Football... *'wherein is nothing but beastlie furie and extreme violence whereof proceedeth hurte, and consequently rancour and malice do remain with them that be wounded'.*

From 'Football' in *Eastern Counties Magazine and Suffolk Note-Book*,
August 1900-May 1901. (Jarrold and Son, 10 and 11 Warwick Lane EC, London)

To be fair, this probably refers to the medieval version of the 'game', a brief description of which is given in our section on 'Diss'.

Following the lads, however, spurred on by the 'First Lady' of Norwich, Delia Smith, is not recommended for folk of a nervous disposition. The glory days were a few short years ago when they spent a giddy year in the Premiership. Then woe and woe again as they were twice relegated. At the time of writing, they are back again vying for top status.

UEA
We must not forget the future of Norwich, in many ways encapsulated by the UEA – the University of East Anglia campus and surrounding countryside which is just a short car or bus ride (24 hour service to and fro, about every 20 minutes) just up the Earlham Road. It is fully open to the public. It is a fine university, rapidly gaining in international distinction, and the choice of many overseas students, especially those from Asia, all of whom bring a refreshing zest to our region. To my mind, the campus is one of the loveliest places on earth. The famous 'ziggurats' of Sir Denys Lasdun stand in front of a lake stocked with fish – I once saw one 'as big as a dog' hurl itself up and out of the water – wildfowl, dragon flies in metallic hues of turquoise and blue, and, in spring and summer, wild plants that delight the senses. You can take many different walks around the lake, along the River Yare for almost as many miles as you like, into the Hardy country of Earlham Park with its ancient oaks and the fattest rabbits in the land hopping all around you, or into adjacent thick woodland.

Some famous people and enterprises:
Norwich has given birth, education or home to many eminent people – among them Herbert de Losinga, Bishop Bathurst (one of 36 children), Edith Cavell, Sir Thomas Bignold, Sir Thomas Ivory, Baroness Amos, Philip Pullman, Admiral Lord Nelson, Sir Thomas Browne, Stephen Fry, Delia Smith, Charles Clarke MP, Kazuo Ishiguro, Ian McEwan, Jeremiah Colman, George Borrow and John Crome. Some famous industries

have started here, too, including Colman's Mustard, Caley's Chocolate, and Boulton and Paul, discussed previously. The UEA , with the motto 'Do Different', has produced an impressive and increasing number of distinguished alumni including Sir Paul Nurse, who won the 2001 Nobel Prize for Physiology or Medicine; Tito Mboweni, present Head of the South African Reserve Bank; Baroness Amos, past Leader of the House of Lords; and Rear Admiral Neil Morisetti, Commander of UK Maritime Forces.

To read: As there is so much to see in every part of town, a specialist book, ideally read before a visit, is highly recommended. The following are on sale in all good bookshops: *Discover Norwich* (Halsgrove) by Stephen Browning – containing 11 walks around the city with historical information, and stories about the people and enterprises in the 'Fine City'. *Norwich* by Daniel Tink (PiXZ Books): a photographic guide to the city.

Winter arrives at the University of East Anglia.

The Spirit of Norwich Cathedral by Daniel Tink and Stephen Browning (PiXZ Books): a guide in words and pictures to the Anglican Cathedral.

To see:
Some essential highlights, which we can unfortunately only just mention here due to lack of space but which are discussed more fully in the above books, include:

The Anglican Cathedral and Close. One of the finest architectural and spiritual treasures of Europe plus a Close of over 44 acres containing 83 Grade 1 or 2 listed buildings.

The Roman Catholic Cathedral of St John the Baptist. A mesmerising and fabulous place, more than anything the vision of one man – Henry, 15th Duke of Norfolk.

The Victorian Plantation Gardens. These beautiful gardens are situated next to the Roman Catholic Cathedral. Often called Norwich's 'secret gardens', they do, indeed, have a magical quality and, as you enter, the 21st century gives way to the 19th. Run entirely by volunteers, you can join the Trust and help out if you like. Else you can simply pay a yearly subscription to help defray costs. Sir Roy Strong is Patron.

The Norman Castle, built to demonstrate who's who after the Conquest.

King Street, once by far the most important street in the city.

St Julian's Shrine. The Church of St Julian is located between King Street and Riverside and the cell of Lady Julian can be visited today. In 1373, recovering from a grave illness, Lady Julian received 16 visitations from God. She subsequently wrote these in the first book to be written in English by a woman, The Revelations of Divine Love, a book, furthermore, which has been in print ever since. She became a recluse and anyone who was troubled was received at her window. Julian would go into the church to pray and, returning, tell the supplicant what the Lord had advised.

Julian taught that there is no anger or hurt in God's love. Here is one saying:

"He says, 'Do not blame yourself too much, thinking that your troubles and distress is all your fault. For it is not my will that you should be unduly sad and despondent.'"

Elm Hill, from eminence to ruin and back again (at least once).

The Market Place, for most citizens the centre of the city.

Chapelfield Gardens – a park in the centre of town dating back centuries: the compulsory archery practice on Sundays would have contributed to the famous victory at Agincourt in 1415 where the commander of the archers was celebrated Norwich citizen, Sir Thomas Erpingham. His effigy can be seen in prayer above the gate to the Anglican Cathedral that bears his name – he is kneeling in prayer, thanking God for having spared his life.

The Great Hospital, founded in 1249 by Walter de Suffield and still doing good today.

Elm Hill – probably the most famous street in Norwich and saved from 'redevelopment by just one council vote in the early twentieth century when it was in a very bad way.

Mousehold Heath – location of Kett's last stand and with fabulous views over the whole city. You can also, like George Borrow, walk for hours on the Heath, most of which is behind you as you look towards the Cathedrals.

Over 30 medieval churches

Pubs – in October 2008, there were still 231 licensed premises in the city to suit every taste.

The Rosary Cemetery. This is a very special place, unknown to most, that encapsulates much of the city's history. It is a five acre plot full of beeches, oaks and chestnuts and, in spring, a mass of bluebells, that is managed with a touch just light enough to keep nature permanently and beautifully on the verge of rampage. In this haven of Victorian peace, only a short distance from the railway station, are buried Jeremiah Colman, John Jarrold, RH Mottram and, more ostentatiously, John Barker, Steam Circus Proprietor, who was killed in an accident on April 12th 1897; along with the great and the good of Victorian society – Norwich Sheriffs, Mayors, artists and important men of industry. It is very tranquil, with the only shock likely to come from a squirrel suddenly springing from one tree branch to another perilously close to your head, almost as if he is playing with you.

University of East Anglia, perfect for study but also incredibly beautiful with the Broad, thick woods and pathways by the River Yare. You will spot lots of fish, wild flowers in hues of yellow, mauve, blue and magenta, dragon flies and (extremely) fat rabbits.

To watch out for: Boundary Markers. These markers can be seen in many parts of the city. David A Berwick, the well-known Norwich historian, says that, from a total of 160 in 1935 there are now, sadly, only about 90 left in the city. What were they for? It was extremely important to mark the exact extent of the parish boundaries as no parish would wish to take on responsibilities that rightly belonged to its neighbours, nor to miss out on the collection of parish rates. 'Walking' the parish limits and putting up Boundary Markers was an often most convivial activity known as 'Beating the Bounds' and involved men and boys, a great quantity of ale usually, plum buns for the boys and maybe a sumptuous dinner for the grown-ups at the end of proceedings. And, to our way of thinking, it could be bizarre. It was not unknown for the maybe muddy party of, say, fifty people to enter a house by the front door and depart through a window if this were the exact parish boundary. Or again, in 1814, Chapelfield Gardens, known then as Chappley Fields, was the city reservoir and the parish boundary went through the lake. A brave swimmer was rewarded with half a crown to swim across it. So that small boys would remember a particular part of a boundary, they were sometimes 'bumped' or

The burial place of John Barker, Steam Circus Proprietor
(Photographed by Stephen Browning).

even hung upside down and their heads 'bumped' – gently we hope! – on the parish edge. Usually the boys would also carry wands of willow and 'beat' the boundary as they proceeded. The following excerpt recalls part of the 'perambulation' – such was one name for it – of Mendlesham in 1898. It is recalled by Mr Walter Tye in 1958:

' The most difficult obstacle encountered in the perambulation was a pig-sty at the Boundary Farm, through which everybody had to clamber, as it laid across the boundary. Entrance by the front gate was easy, but squeezing through the small muck-hole at the back was indeed trying, especially to the more corpulent farmers. Anyhow, with assistance both fore and aft, everybody managed to squeeze through. Most likely the expectancy of hospitality in the farm kitchen made everybody all the keener. And we were not disappointed. Never were ham sandwiches, pork pies, Suffolk rusks and home-brewed beer more relished. The beer, so said our host, was brewed on the day his eldest son was born, and he was in his teens. Despite caution, however, many of the thirsty 'beaters' were afterwards found sleeping it off in a haystack....

....There were no absentees, however, at the Royal Oak Inn later in the day, when a sumptuous supper was laid out on long tables in an upper room. There before us were huge joints of beef and mutton, tasty pies, bowls of vegetables and salads, cakes of every description, and scores of shaky tinted jellies, the likes of which we seldom see today. Even if the aged Rector had failed to bless the crops during the day he certainly had no compunction in giving thanks for such a welcome spread. Supper was followed by speeches, songs, tales and jokes, most of which we had heard before, and of which we never tired. Farmers, tradesmen, millers, shoemakers all took part, until we heard that oft repeated call. 'Time, gentlemen, please'. One and all agreed that 'beating the bounds' was a fine institution and should long continue. But alas, with the passage of time, this ancient custom is well nigh forgotten, the Royal Oak Inn is no more and only a few of the old Mendlesham 'beaters' are left to tell the tale'

For further information please see: Beating the Bounds in Georgian Norwich by David A Berwick (the Larks Press): a guide to a fascinating ancient custom which can lead you around the extant boundary markers of the city.

Don't ask: There are two things you must not ask in a local pub if you wish to continue your drink in peace:

1.   'Have you guys got a football team?'
2.   'Doesn't Jamie Oliver, the famous chef, live around here?'

Ormesby St Margaret with Scratby

With a population a little over 4000, Ormesby St Margaret with Scratby are adjacent popular seaside resorts, situated about 6 miles north of Great Yarmouth. Usually, people add 'and California' which makes quite a long name! California is so named because, in May 1848, a collection of sixteenth century gold coins was found near the cliffs. During the next few years when people founded the new village, the California Gold Rush was very much in the news and it was decided to use the American name for the Norfolk settlement which numbered 40 houses by 1870.

To do: the main attraction of the area are the wonderful sandy beaches. There are a few shops, fish and chips and Chinese take-aways and the area is quiet and perfect for families. Self-catering cottages are easily available.

The sandy beach at Scratby.

Walkers explore the Norfolk Coast Path at Blakeney.

Peddars Way

Running from Knettishall Heath Country Park in Suffolk to Holmes-next-the-sea on the North Norfolk Coast, this is a fantastic way to explore the countryside by walking (the name derives from the Latin word 'pedester' which means 'on foot'). At Holmes-next-the-sea it meets the Norfolk Coast Path which runs from Hunstanton to Cromer. The whole route is over 93 miles long if the Norfolk Coast Path is included, but can be tackled by sections – for example, Little Cressingham to Castle Acre (11.7 miles) or Burnham Overy Staithe to Stiffkey (9.8 miles). Large parts can also be travelled on horseback or by bicycle. The Ordnance Survey publishes a detailed guide.

The Norfolk Coast Path from Sheringham to Cromer.

A wander through Overstand village.

The beach at Overstrand looking towards Cromer Pier.

Poppyland

The power of the pen

'Poppyland' was the term made up by Clement Scott who worked for the *Daily Telegraph* and in 1883 arrived in Overstrand – he had come to cover the Cromer area for his readers as, since the coming of the railway several years before, the North Norfolk Coast was fast becoming *the* place to holiday. He instantly fell in love with the area. He wrote prolifically and Overstrand's fame grew.

Soon, the 'great and the good' from London were vying with each other to build a grand summer home in Overstrand. It became probably the most exclusive village in the Kingdom – the list of visitors and house builders includes Sir Henry Irving, Swinburne, Lord Morley, Lord Wolverhampton and Sir Edward MacMillan. In 1898 Edwin Lutyens designed The Pleasance for Baron Hillingdon – Lutyens was only 29 and the design, although striking and original, remained controversial. Overstrand gained its own railway station.

In 1903, the Overstrand Hotel, designed by Boardman and Son of Norwich, opened its very grand doors. Sadly, it was built too close to the edge of the cliffs and was never completely secure. In 1947 a fire ended the story.

Now, Overstrand is much smaller and the railway is gone. But it has some extraordinary memories.

Beware: In the late 19th and early 20th Century it was believed that the 'lantern men' were abundant in the area from Overstrand to Cromer. They came out of the ground as vapours and chased you. If they caught you, they would kill so the thing to do was to throw yourself onto the ground and hold your breath for as long as possible. They seem to have something in common with the Death Eaters in the Harry Potter books.

Rockland St Mary

This is classic 'watery walking' Norfolk, as well as a haven for pleasure boats at Rockland Staithe. Part of the area's appeal is the low density of population which makes rambling a pleasure. There is a marvellous walk taking in Rockland St Mary, the adjacent village of Surlingham and the incomparable Ted Ellis Nature Reserve.

To do: There is a Buddhist Community and Retreat Centre at Surlingham (Friends of the Western Buddhist Order) who organise retreats for weekends, weeks or fortnights at Lessingham House and there is always lots of time left free to explore the area. Fees are quite moderate, the food vegetarian.

Cycling is also easy, the land being pretty flat.

To see: Rockland St Mary Church is an attractive mish-mash of Tudor (maybe a little older in parts) and Victorian styles.

Beyond the reed beds is Rockland St Mary broad.

The Church of St Peter and St Paul in Salle.

Salle

Against his will
Here lies George Hill,
Who from a cliff
Fell down quite stiff

Epitaph in Church of St Peter and St Paul

Salle – pronounced to rhyme with 'call' – is a tiny, cute-as-can-be village a little to the north of Dereham. There is a magnificent church set in barley fields alongside a cricket pitch.

There is a somewhat macabre legend, however, regarding the fate of the beheaded body of Anne Boleyn. Some say that her body was buried in the churchyard here in 1536, but without the heart which was cut out and later discovered in a church wall at Thetford, whence it was returned to St Peter and St Paul. According to local legend, each 19th May, the anniversary of her execution, an aggrieved Anne - holding her bloody head - can be seen sometimes here and sometimes at nearby Blickling Hall.

Salthouse

The salt of the earth
Salt was once a very precious commodity and Salthouse lies on the salt marshes of North Norfolk in an Area of Outstanding Natural Beauty. Seven hundred years ago there were more salt pans here than anywhere else in Britain. The salt water would be boiled, the resulting salt fashioned into blocks and then stored here until needed by the nobility or wealthy merchants. Quite evidently, it was a place to be reckoned with.

'Kiss me…Myngs??'
A famous citizen was Sir Christopher Myngs, baptised on 22 November 1625. He was one of the county's most loved seamen who lost his life in valiant fashion in an action against the troublesome Dutch in 1666. We have a record of his funeral from Pepys who records that a dozen of his men were grief stricken to the extent of begging the King for a fireship in order to seek revenge. We don't know if this was granted directly, probably not, but the war with the Dutch was to continue for many a year and Norfolk seamen were at the forefront of innumerable brave actions.

Don't build your house on sand
Another eminent local of very different hue was a man who made his fortune in London property before retiring to Salthouse. He revelled in the magnificent name of Onesiphorous (it means roughly 'making money') Randall. And he built a castle. On the

The pebbled coastline and waters at Salthouse are popular with fishermen.

beach. He had a cannon placed in front to keep away unwelcome prying eyes for his carriage was reported to often be seen whisking along the sands towards his domain in the late evening carrying a beautiful lady. He died in 1873 when the 'Folly', as it was known, was sold and used by the Coastguards. In the Second World War it was utilised for military purposes until the whole thing was carried away by the sea in 1953.

To do: The Salthouse Sculpture Trail is a 10 mile trail around the village that takes in birdwatching, wildlife, woodland and pubs. The Greater Spotted Woodpecker can be seen here as well as some lovely dragonflies. If your legs tire, part of the trail – Holt to Kelling Heath Holt - can be made on the North Norfolk Poppy Line.

Each year there is an exhibition of local artists, rapidly gaining in national and international repute, organised by the North Norfolk Education Project.

Contact: Salthouse may not be very big but it has a thriving website to which potential visitors can address queries – www.salthousehistory.co.uk

Be careful what you ask for: you may get an unusual look if, during your guesthouse breakfast you ask, 'Have you any salt, please?'

Will you come for an evening walk amongst he salt marshes of Salthouse?

Bird watchers visit Salthouse in great numbers to spot rare species.

War memorial at Sandringham.

Sandringham

This royal estate was bought in 1861 for the Prince of Wales by his mother, Queen Victoria. The church of St Mary Magdalene is the home church of Her Majesty Queen Elizabeth II and other members of the Royal Family.

At one time, the top-performing boy each year at my school, King Edward VII Grammar School in King's Lynn, used to come here to receive a gold medal from King Edward VII himself.

I remember as a schoolboy running cross country races around here: I hated the racing but have never forgotten the glorious woodland we stumbled and splashed through.

To see: The House - most of the ground floor rooms used by the Royal Family are open to the public.

To walk around: There are sixty acres of utterly gorgeous gardens to explore, as beautiful in Autumn as in Spring and Summer. You will never see more fabulous rhododendrons in hues of magenta, lemon, snowy white, pink and lavender.

Sandringham Country Park is open daily and has some glorious wooded walks.

The lovely Sea Palling beach from the sand dunes.

Sea Palling

Sea Palling has always been battered by the sea, many lives having been lost over the centuries. In 1995 the government launched a multi-million pound project, erecting nine barrier reefs. In the 16th and 17th centuries the rough seas also provided an income of sorts as ships in distress were plundered.

Today, never quite tamed, it provides a fine example of unspoilt Norfolk beauty. The beaches are flat and sandy, popular in calm weather with jet skiers.

Defensive rocks protect the sandy beach, cliffs and dunes at Sea Palling.

113

Sheringham

'Once a sleepy Norfolk fishing village, Sheringham was transformed by the arrival of the railway in 1887 and grew over the years into a thriving holiday town with safe golden beaches and a beautiful hinterland. Grand Victorian houses sprang up and the town assumed an air of gentility enjoyed by the 'Great and the Good' who had 'discovered' Sheringham and its easy way of life. The twentieth century saw greater numbers arrive, while the public taste for seaside holidays was encouraged through ease of access via the railway with visitor comforts accommodated by hotels and guesthouses. And throughout all the changes down the years the town has retained a strong sense of identity and today retains pride in the title of 'The Premier Resort on the North Norfolk Coast".

The Book of Sheringham by Peter Brooks (Halsgrove 2009)

Sheringham beach huts at sunset.

*Poppies in a field below
Beeston Bump.*

For anyone wanting a 'taste' of the true Sheringham, the book from which the above quote is taken, will certainly not disappoint as Mr Brooks has an unrivalled knowledge of and love for the town, and his writing is always entertaining. An impartial observer cannot help but smile, though, as the last sentence underlines the fierce rivalry of the many resorts on the North Norfolk Coast. In particular, you are either a Sheringham or a Cromer man: you must choose. Earlier in these pages, I put the Cromer side of the argument.

There was once a Lower and an Upper Sheringham, but today the town is centred around a thriving high street which has an interesting array of shops which include art and craft shops, antiques and books and, naturally, fishing tackle and bait specialists. Although cod and herring fishing has declined enormously, Sheringham is still well known as an idyllic spot to try your luck, as well as a centre for crabs, lobsters and whelks. Sheringham lifeboats have saved many lives over the years and they have been dragged into position by tractor and launched from the beach, there being no raised harbour to facilitate a spectacular launch.

To see: St Joseph Roman Catholic Church, designed by Sir Giles Gilbert Scott, is a listed building which celebrated its centenary in 2008. It looks a little like an industrial building which is rare amongst Norfolk churches but typical of the architect's style.

The original 1867 RNLI Lifeboat station, Oddfellows Hall, has been totally refurbished and is designed to be used by the community for all manner of meetings.

Beeston Bump can be accessed via Peddars Way and North Norfolk Coastal Path.

*A wonderful view of
Sheringham from
Beeston Bump.*

117

To walk: The land to the rear of the town is wonderful walking country. A leaflet of suggested 'Sheringham Trails' is available from the tourist office. Keep an eye out for Adders, particularly if you have a dog with you as they don't appreciate being harassed. They are generally harmless, however, if left alone.

Beware: The Yow-Yows. These are ghosts of sailors who drowned off the Sheringham coast. If you hear their cries, it means a storm is coming and it is best to get off the beach: when the wind is at its height they will wail loudest, hoping to lure some more sailors to join them at the bottom of the ocean.

Black Shuk: This throat-tearing huge dog, according to legend, operates hereabouts. Some claim that reports of savagery by the hound have been invented to scare away outsiders and that it is, in fact, a gentle creature who, since 1709 has been morosely searching for his shipwrecked master. If this is the case, I don't know how to account for the chilling story by Christopher Marlowe in our section on 'Cromer'.

Snettisham

The village of Snettisham has a nature reserve in the care of the Royal Society for the Protection of Birds. Here you will see Wading birds, Pinkfooted Geese by the thousand, Terns and Black-headed Gulls. There is no time during the year that is other than fantastic for the bird lover.

St Mary's Church in Snettisham can be seen miles away, thanks to its impressive spire.

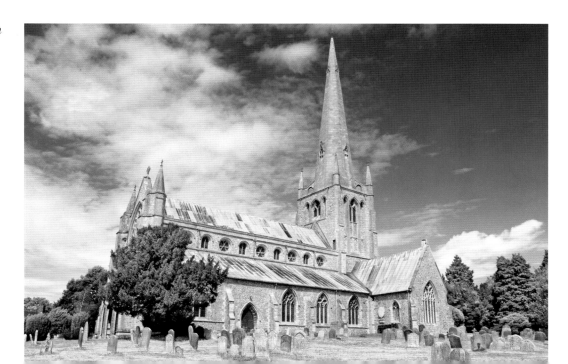

Neighbouring the beach at Snettisham are some fabulous walks.

Snettisham is known locally as the point where 'Norfolk stares at Lincolnshire'; this is because it is on the west coast of Norfolk and thus faces Lincolnshire which is only 15 miles distant.

Please be careful: with your dogs and keep them to the bridleways and footpaths.

Swaffham

'Here lies the body of Thomas Parr.
What, Old Tom? No.
What, Young Tom? Ah.'
Epitaph in Swaffham Church (from *East Anglian Epitaphs*,
Raymond Lamont-Brown, Acorn Editions 1981)

The legend of John Chapman
The story goes that Swaffham Church was paid for entirely by a pedlar, John Chapman, who dreamed that if he made his way to London Bridge, something wonderful would be told to him. He made his way to London with great difficulty – this was in the 16th century and he had no money – where he stood on London Bridge for some hours until a man came up to him and asked him what he was doing there. John Chapman told the truth – he was, he said, obeying the instructions in a dream. The other scoffed and said what a foolish thing it was to believe in dreams. ' For if I was as stoop-ud as thee, I would believe a dream I have just had in which I was told that a man, called John Chapman from a town called Swaffham in the county of Norfolk has a tree in his garden under

The 'Butter Cross' is found in the market place of Swaffham.

*The church of St Peter and
St Paul in Swaffham – but who
paid for such an imposing place
of worship?*

which is a pot of money. Fooey! Thou art a siller owld fule!' As fast as he could, John Chapman scurried back home to Swaffham and dug under the tree in his garden. Lo! There was a box - but it was empty. On the lid was a Latin inscription which, not understanding, he placed in his front window. Presently some learned scholars came walking by and in voices John Chapman could hear, translated the inscription:

> *'Under me doth lie
> Another much richer than I.'*

He dug again, and deeper. He discovered a great treasure and, to show his gratitude to God, he paid the entire cost of building the church.

The church itself is magnificent, built largely of Barnack stone which was expensive: whoever paid for it – and I would like to believe every word of the legend – was very wealthy.

The *place to be seen*
Many Norfolk villages and town have had their 'moment in the sun', so to speak, but Swaffham's was more spectacular than your average. In the late 18th and early 19th Centuries it was no less than a social centre to rival almost anywhere on the Continent. Its fine houses and finer roads welcomed the aristocracy to balls, soirées and concerts:

The war memorial in Swaffham.

aristocratic parents would bring their daughters here ' for the season' and hope thereby to gain a suitable husband. Lord Orford is reputed to have raced his greyhounds around the countryside known as the Brecks, adjacent to the town, and thus founded the sport. A pub in the town is called The Greyhound Inn and it was here that his Lordship founded the first coursing club in 1776.

Visitors are sometimes surprised by the quality of the town's houses but that is because the finest date from this period. Much of the hit TV series *The Kingdom*, starring Stephen Fry, was filmed here (The Greyhound Inn becoming The Startled Duck in the series).

A legendary resident was Howard Carter who uncovered the tomb of Tutankhamun. Another was Sir Arthur Knyvet Wilson, one of a very few Royal Navy officers to win the Victoria Cross. He was born in the town in 1842 and died there in 1921, his last job having been to help lead the Navy through the First World War. Not as famous Nelson, but arguably almost as significant.

To do: Just wandering around the town is very nice. If you like cycling, a leaflet is available in the town which will guide you round the Brecks Cycling Discovery Route. Similar trails exist for horse riders.

Swanton Morley

This very pretty village, situated in the heart of Norfolk, has an unrivalled historical claim to fame. Young Samuel Lincoln, left penniless due to family disputes, fled to Hingham, Massachusetts. His great-great-great-great grandson was Abraham Lincoln, President of the United States.

Don't say: when meeting a visitor from the United States, of which there are quite a few who come back to trace family history, 'And how *is* life in the colonies?'

All Saints Church, Swanton Morley.

Beyond the graveyard at All Saints Church is the stunning Wensum valley.

Swardeston

This small village, south of Norwich, was the birthplace of Edith Cavell who, as a nurse in occupied Belgium, established an escape route for wounded Allied soldiers. She was arrested in 1915, tried entirely in German which she didn't speak, and shot in 1915. The night before her death she famously remarked that 'patriotism is not enough' as she would willingly have helped soldiers of any nationality. She was brought home with great (and royal) fanfare after the War and now lies in Life's Green, a beautiful spot alongside Norwich Cathedral.

Her father, the Revd Frederick Cavell was also a remarkable man in his own right and, in his frugality, typical of many East Anglians. He was vicar of St Mary's Church in the village for 45 years. He thought hardship good as it kept out the devil; besides, life was certainly not to be enjoyed as we were all here to serve a higher purpose.

Swardeston has a very fine cricket team, regularly winning the highest Norfolk honours.

Thetford

'Its history has been a chequered one. From the days before written history began to the time of the Crusades, Thetford's record was one of progress, not uninterrupted, but with periods of retrogression, yet on the whole of undeniable progress. From the time of the Crusades Thetford's history has been in the main a record of decadence. Spasmodic efforts have been made to recover some of the old prestige, succeeded, however, by the ultimately prevalent apathy and indifference.'

There are some wonderful views of Thetford from Castle Hill.

An assessment of Thetford about 1900 , taken from Eastern Counties Magazine and Suffolk Note-Book, August 1900-May 1901 (Jarrold and Son, 10 and 11 Warwick Lane EC, London)

'If we do not hang together, we shall surely hang separately'

Thomas Paine

A fascinating historical mix
Few market towns the size of Thetford can boast such an interesting past and present. In AD 60 it was the seat of Boudica; In the mid ninth Century the miracle of Saint Edmund

occurred; in the 18th Century the thoughts and writings of Thetford resident, Thomas Paine, were highly influential in the rebellion of the American colonies; today, it is at the forefront of multi-culturalism in Britain and has become home to large numbers of people from eastern Europe and Portugal – an estimated 6-7,000 people have Portuguese as their first language. When England play Portugal at football, international relations can be just a touch testy.

Boudica and daughters
Boudica was the wife of Prasutagus, King of the Iceni people who populated Norfolk in the first half of the 1st Century. When he died, he left the Kingdom jointly to the Roman Emperor and his daughters. This could have been a clever move because normally the Romans simply took a kingdom into the Empire as soon as the client king died and here was an attempt to willingly give up half his kingdom if his family could keep the other half. The Romans, however, were unimpressed, especially as Prasutagus had what we today would call a ruinous 'overdraft' courtesy of Rome – he had been living beyond his means for years. The loans were called in and could not be paid. Boudica was flogged for such audacity and her daughters raped.

Boudica was by all accounts a tall woman with flowing red hair and a penetrating voice. She has been depicted as wearing a multi-coloured robe and was very bright. She led the Iceni people into Colchester and sacked it, before routing the Roman legion sent to relieve it. She next turned her attention to London, only to have the Roman commander, Suetonius, order its abandonment as he did not have the forces to defend it. She burnt it to the ground anyway. In all, maybe 80,000 people – her fellow citizens as well as the Roman invaders – were put to death in horrific ways, as Boudica had no truck with the expense of keeping prisoners. Suetonius regrouped his forces and proved far too canny a battle commander for Boudica whose army was decimated. Historians think this was probably in the West Midlands. The romantic version of events has her taking her own life so that she would not be captured, while other reports say she just died.

The interesting thing about all this is that the stories of her come from Rome, as no-one in Britain was in a position to write a report. This may be why her legend, so strong now, was forgotten for centuries and only became a part of British folklore when Queen Victoria was seen as her 'namesake'. The wonderful statue of her in a chariot, with swords whirring on the wheels, as she presumably leads the route of a Roman legion, is situated outside the Houses of Parliament in London, and is a fanciful work commissioned by Prince Albert, executed by Thomas Thorneycroft. She did, after all, kill far more of her own people than the hated Romans.

Thetford continued to be important in the centuries that followed as the 'Thetford

A floating restaurant and geese on the Little Ouse River at Thetford.

Treasure' – spoons, gold rings, pendants and a gold buckle, discovered in 1979 and now in the possession of the British Museum – bears witness. Castle Hill in the south of the town is the largest Norman motte in England, although all traces of the Castle have vanished as it was likely made of wood. Its importance declined relatively when Herbert de Losinga moved the centre of the See to Norwich, and laid the foundation stone of Norwich Cathedral, at the instigation of the Pope, in 1094.

St Edmund's head and the wolf
Thetford was also the home of Edmund, crowned King of the East Anglians in 856. The story goes that, after the Danes had invaded his kingdom and defeated Edmund, he was offered his life in return for renouncing God. He refused, was tied to a tree, his body shot full of arrows and he was beheaded. His body and head were scandalously thrown into the thick wood of Hoxne without any respect. After the Danes had left, the heartbroken people of East Anglia rounded up all the men they could find to help recover Edmund's remains. His body was soon found but, not being able to find the head, one of the men called out, 'Where are you?' A voice answered, 'I am here. Here!' Upon investigation they found Edmund's head being guarded between the forefeet of a wolf. The wolf released the head and accompanied the men back to the place where Edmund's body lay. The head united itself precisely with the body. The wolf returned to the forest.

Reason or treason?
Thomas Paine's father kept a shop in Thetford selling women's underwear. His illustrious son's famous book *The Rights of Man* was written in defence of the French Revolution and infuriated the already nervous powers-that-be in England as well as encouraging resistance to all things English in America. Surely, people thought, here was an act of treason? Thomas Paine presented his thoughts as the result of reason and tolerance. Naotaro Kudo, a visiting Professor of Philosophy of Religion from Waseda University, Tokyo, visited East Anglia and fell in love with the area. In 1976 he published a marvellous book, *A Stranger in East Anglia* (East Anglian Magazine Ltd), surely more than anything a love letter to the area, in which he remarked that, though espousing reason to others, Thomas Paine undoubtedly lacked it himself. This may explain why he died without any money in New York in 1809 and why it took until 1964 for a statue to be erected to him in his home town.

To visit: The 'Thetford Treasure' in the British Museum, London.

To see: Castle Hill motte in the town – from the top of the mound is a fine vista of the surrounding area.

To do: The adjacent Thetford Forest is the largest – and man-made – lowland pine forest

On Butten Island stands the impressive bronze statue of Duleep Singh, the last Maharajah of the Punjab, who settled close to Thetford.

in the Kingdom. The government planted it following the First World War. You can cycle and walk almost all over and there is a Visitors' Centre with café etc in the middle. Bikes can be hired here.

There is even 'Music in the Forest' in clement weather by both pop and classical artists. In winter Husky racing takes place.

To spot: It is not surprising that such a thick forest provides shelter for endangered birds such as the Crossbill, Siskin, Nightjar and others.

Don't do: Don't go tripping about without a guide as you'll likely get shot – the Army uses parts of the forest for training purposes.

Thornham

Beaches, oysters and butterflies
Thornham has changed greatly in the last two hundred years. The population was around 800 in the mid 19th Century but today there are, perhaps, 200 fully occupied and owned properties – the rest are holiday homes. Tourism and oysters are major money-spinners.

Nobody knows for sure the purpose of the famous old stumps in the harbour, but they look as if they had a defensive purpose. If you walk from the harbour to the beach you will see many more modern posts on the beach, the function of which is to delay erosion of the sand dunes which are such a lovely feature of the area.

The walk from Thornham Harbour to the beach is long but the views along the way are well worth the effort.

An old wrecked boat sits resignedly in the marsh at Thornham.

127

The coal barn is a well-known landmark in Thornham.

The famous Thornham Stumps.

This is butterfly heaven, with Large Whites, Peacocks and Red Admirals.

All Saints Church is larger than you might expect and dates back to the 13th century.

Thurne

Water and walks

A lovely Norfolk Broads community, Thurne also offers walking to suit everyone: the Weavers Way passes through the village. There is also a fine old church and well-known local pottery.

Thurne Mill on a blustery day.

Would you ever forget a walk
along the riverside at Thurne?

Walsingham

'On our left we see Walsingham, an ancient town, famous for the old ruins of a monastery of note there,
and the shrine of our lady, as noted as that of Sir Thomas-a-Becket at Canterbury, and for little else'
Daniel Defoe, Tour through the Eastern Counties, first published 1724.
(New edition East Anglian Magazine Ltd 1949.)

Lady Richeldis has a vision
In a vision in 1061, Lady Richeldis, who owned Walsingham Manor, was transported to
Nazareth by the Virgin Mary, shown the house where Jesus was born and told to build a

Little Walsingham is a quintessential Norfolk village.

replica in Walsingham. Thus she built a simple structure of wood and, afterwards, a priory was also built. It was really special. Erasmus visited in 1511 and said : 'You will say it is the seat of the gods, so bright and shining as it is all over with jewels, gold and silver'.

Which is probably why Henry VIII plundered it in 1538. The Prior, one Richard Vowell, was complicit in handing over the treasures to Henry and destroying the structure, for which his 'forty pieces of silver' was a pension to the vast tune of 100 pounds a year. *The Walsingham Lament*, written at this time, comments like this:

> *Weepe, weepe, O Walsingham,*
> *Whose dayes are nights,*
> *Blessings turned to blasphemies,*
> *Holy deeds to dispites.*
> *Sinne is where our Ladye sate,*
> *Heaven turned is to helle;*
> *Satan sitthe where our Lord did swaye,*
> *Walsingham O farewell!*

For 300 years the site was left in ruins. However, in 1897 it was extensively restored and in 1931 a replica of Lady Richeldis' shrine was rebuilt. It immediately became, and remains, a place of pilgrimage for thousands. You can get here by steam railway from Wells-next-the-sea.

Looking down the historic High Street in Little Walsingham.

The timber-framed Oxford Stores Inn at Little Walsingham.

Wells-next-the-Sea

Arising from a spring

The name derives from *Wella*, Latin for a spring, of which the area had many. In the 16th Century it was a very important port, indeed, but the harbour has since silted up and the town is presently a mile inland. The name Wells-next-the-sea was adopted officially in the 1950s to distinguish the town from others whose name derives from the same source.

The town now mainly earns its living from tourism and has a long, sandy beach with sand dunes providing lots of fun for the little ones. Boating takes place in a pool called Abraham's Bosom. At the rear of the beach, planted in the sand, are dense woods – mainly Scots and Corsican Pine.

To see: The town itself is pretty and mainly Georgian. At the centre is The Buttlands, a green, and the Catholic Church.

The fine Albatross *sailing ship moored at Wells-next-the-Sea Harbour was built in Rotterdam in 1899.*

Colourful beach huts at Wells-next-the-Sea cast shadows on a sunny beach, late afternoon.

The lifeboat station can be seen in the harbour,

To do: One cannot help wonder how Wells, as is the case with many settlements on the North Norfolk Coast, would have fared had it been able to hide from Dr Beeching who closed down its remaining railway station in the 1960s. Railway enthusiasts will, however, be fascinated both by the Wells and Walsingham Light Railway and the Wells Harbour Railway, both 10 and a quarter inch gauge.

Hundreds of Pink-footed Geese fly past Wells-next-the-Sea in the evening looking to roost. At dawn they will fly inland to feed on arable fields. This awesome spectacle occurs in winter when 150,000 geese migrate to Norfolk from Iceland and Greenland.

*Wells-next-the-Sea Harbour with
the noted Granary landmark.*

West Runton

By Daniel Tink

As the photographer for this book I thought it would be nice to write a few words on a place that holds many special memories for me from my childhood summer holidays. The Runtons, East and West, are quaint villages on the North Norfolk Coast between Cromer and Sheringham.

West Runton has become a family favourite throughout the summer months, with long stretches of unspoilt beaches. Sandy in a few places, regular visitors will notice an occasional change in the way the shoreline appears, thanks to where the tide decides to position the numerous collections of stones and seaweed patches, which will sometimes lead to a slightly further walk to find that perfect bump-free spot for your picnic blanket.

The glorious view of West Runton village from nearby Incleborough Hill.

A common scenario that makes me smile is watching families pack on to the hard sands that appear when the tide is out, to then have to dash back to the drier but stonier sands when the inevitable happens. Most will make it, but some only realise at the last minute

After sunset on the beach at West Runton – groynes disappear into the distance towards Sheringham.

and end up taking home slightly salty and damp possessions. The more sensible (and no doubt West Runton regulars) will have sourced the best sandy positions safe from the tide earlier in the day.

West Runton has been our family holiday destination for many years, always timing it to coincide with Cromer Carnival week in August. I recall great numbers of the family creating a huge arc of windbreaks. It was indeed behind the windbreaks where I used to get up to great mischief. I remember quietly positioning myself behind my poor Dad and attempting to dig under the windbreak and his deck chair in hope of a sudden tip backwards! Another fun game was digging a hole where somebody had been sitting on their towel, placing the towel back over the top and waiting for my next victim. Now I'm 29 I look back and realise how much of a tease I was! (But it was fun all the same).

Family fun on the beach at West Runton.

During low tide, the sea will slowly reveal a hidden landscape that starts with exposure of a few rock pools and extends into crabbing heaven for some – brave beginners beware of sharp pinchers! On an exceptionally low scouring tide you are treated to an ancient

West Runton village from the main Norfolk Norfolk coast road.

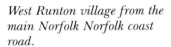

foreshore of chalk, clay and rock formations. On closer inspection you will find an abundance of sea creatures, both live and fossilised dating back to Jurassic and Cretaceous periods – Belemnites are a common find (these are shaped like a bullet).

Fossils can also be found in exposed areas of the cliff known as the Cromer Forest Bed (which dates back some 500,000–700,000 years ago). Indeed, it was the discovery of a very special find in the early 1990s that put West Runton high on the geological map. After a particularly stormy winter night, fossilised remains of a large pelvic bone were discovered. Over the next few years as more bones were uncovered it became clear that a major find may be on the cards. An excavation soon revealed the largest and most complete elephant skeleton to date. Now known famously as the 'West Runton Elephant' the species was a ten ton Steppe Mammoth that dated back some 700,000 years. A few of the bones can be seen on display at Cromer museum. Photos and text from the excavation can be seen in the West Runton beach Café.

The popularity of the Runtons has grown over the years and it's easy to see why - safe and fun family beaches, pretty villages and a convenient place to stay whilst exploring the North Norfolk coast; whilst for me, as a landscape photographer, there is nowhere more beautiful.

To do: Walk to Sheringham along the cliff top, pausing for a time at the top of Beeston Bump for a welcome rest with some stunning views of West Runton and Sheringham – particularly special at sunset. Alternatively walk the other direction to East Runton and eventually Cromer (approximately 2 miles).

On the beach, try crabbing in the rock pools or hunt for fossils. If you have a sweet tooth I can highly recommend the flapjack from the Beach Café.

Away from the beach and near the main road, the Village Inn, with its large garden, is an ideal spot for a refreshing drink, and it serves some inexpensive tasty meals, too.

If you love horses then don't miss the Shire Horse Centre with Shire-Horse pulled rides or take a guided trek out into the local countryside.

To see: Visit the beach during Cromer Carnival Week during August (usually on a Wednesday) and you will be treated to the spectacular Red Arrows as they perform amazing stunts and tricks and swoop low over the sea.

Weybourne

He who would all England win, should at Weybourne Hope begin
Old English saying

Weybourne – pronounced Webbon, as along with much of Norfolk the village refuses to comply with the generally accepted rules of the English language – has very deep water offshore, meaning ships would be able to dock very close to land: hence the above saying. There was much concern in 1588 when the Spanish Armada was imminently expected. During the Second World War there were landmines, pillboxes, anti-tank ditches and acres of barbed wire along this coastal stretch. A controlled zone was established which

Walkers take an early morning stroll along the cliff tops at Weybourne.

139

A stormy sunrise at Weybourne.

extended 10 miles deep into the North Sea. There was also the top-secret Weybourne Camp, specialising in anti-aircraft matters, and this received two visits by Winston Churchill just after Dunkirk. In scenes that sound as if they come straight out of Dad's Army, the missile firing demonstration was pretty hopeless – during the second visit, a pilotless aircraft was successfully shot down but almost landed on top of the assembled VIPs. An enraged PM immediately sacked the top command.

Dad's Army did, indeed, subsequently come here to film – the beautiful Weybourne Station was the setting for the episode 'The Royal Train.' The station, just outside the village centre, is on the 'Poppy Line' running from Sheringham to Holt and a ride will take you on a ten mile round trip amongst some of the most fabulous scenery in the county and the country. The area is awash with tale of smuggling and derring-do. The name of the village means 'felon's stream' which gives a clue its ancient reputation: it was probably the stretch of water in which convicted criminals were drowned. Many Norfolk villages had a stream for such a specific purpose. Valuable quantities of gin, brandy and tobacco were sometimes landed, sometimes seized, much depending on the co-operation or otherwise of the locals. If you lived near the beach and turned a blind eye to night-time goings-on, you would likely find a nice 'present' left on your doorstep the next morning.

To do: This is an ideal location to book a hotel if you like peace and quiet and want easy access to the North Norfolk Coast. Local attractions include Sheringham Park, planted in the 19th Century with rhododendrons and azaleas only equalled in beauty by the gardens at Sandringham. The beach is of pebbles and thus ideal for anglers if not swimmers – the sands of Sheringham are only about three miles away. As always along the North Norfolk Coast, bring your binoculars and a good book for identifying the dozens of species of birds which roost, nest, whirl and whoop all over.

There's the Muckleburgh Collection on the outskirts, too, but we cover that in a separate section.

Winterton-on-Sea

This is a small – population is under 1500 – village beloved of those who seek time to stand still. It is 8 miles to the north of Great Yarmouth on the Norfolk Coast and famous for the Winterton Dunes which lie between the village and the coast and where you can see the Natterjack Toad. Seals can be observed at Duffles Pond. Efforts to stabilize the coast against the perpetual threat of sea encroachment have been made since at least the 18th Century when an enlightened programme of marram grass planting was begun. It is, though, an ongoing threat.

Golden sands at Winterton stretch for miles along Norfolk's east coast.

The dunes at Winterton provide marvellous scenic views.

To do: The long beach is a paradise for children – much like Hunstanton, pools form on the beach which always yield some treasure or fascination to eager young eyes.

The Church of the Holy Trinity and All Saints has a fine tower.

Nightlife is easily sorted out – there is one pub, the Fisherman's Return.

Wymondham

Buried in Wymondham church is a man called None: he gave nothing to the Monastery during his lifetime and the English translation of a Latin verse satirizing him reads:

> *Here lies None, one worse than none for ever thought,*
> *And because None, of None to Thee, O Christ, gives nought.*
> *None lieth here, of Linage none descended,*
> *Amongst men none, None 'mongst the Saints befriended.*

From: *Wymondham Old and New* by JEG Mosby SSO and PE Agar
(Geo R. Reeve, The Model Press, Wymondham, Norfolk 1949)

Just punishments

The most famous resident of Wymondham was Robert Kett, who was hanged in chains outside Norwich Castle for leading a rebellion against King Edward 1st in 1549. We

Market Cross in the centre of Wymondham.

would probably regard him as an ordinary – tho' educated chap – who resisted the unreasonable, life-threatening, enclosures of land by the nobility. For centuries, people had been able to graze their livestock, and generally enjoy, the 'common lands' in the county. Suddenly these lands became private property. We would all want a champion, wouldn't we?

The modern idea of prisons dates from here: in 1785 John Howard suggested a prison system where inmates had their own cell. This is now universally accepted in the free world. Now, the Headquarters of the Norfolk Constabulary is based here.

Market Street in Wymondham as the very early sun peeps around the far bend.

*Sheep may safely graze
Wymondham Abbey.*